Philip Mallet
Mary Mallet.

Fancy Free in Baghdad, Letters From Mary Borlase to her Parents 1950-1952

Fancy Free in Baghdad
Letters from Mary Borlase
to her Parents 1950-1952

Edited by

PHILIP MALLET

The Memoir Club

© Philip Mallet 2003

First published in 2003 by
The Memoir Club
Whitworth Hall
Spennymoor
County Durham

British Library Cataloguing in
Publication Data.
A catalogue record for this book
is available from the
British Library.

ISBN: 1 84104 083 5

Typeset by George Wishart & Associates, Whitley Bay.
Printed by Bookcraft (Bath) Ltd.

*In loving memory of
Granville and Marjorie Borlase,
the recipients of these letters.*

Contents

Illustrations

Introduction

I SUPPOSE IT WAS fairly grim to be brought up in wartime Britain, though it seemed pretty normal when you had known nothing else. After the war rationing and austerity persisted, but the atmosphere lightened; and one way to have fun and see life was to get a job abroad.

Mary Borlase was born in 1930. Her upbringing in a country rectory and in a girls' boarding school must have been fairly sheltered. She had no call to be a bluestocking, and in any case her parents would have found it hard to support her at university, so she took a secretarial course after leaving school. Then with the help of her godfather who was an army officer, she got a job in what was then known as a branch of the War Office, and which now stands revealed as M.I.5 or the Security Service. After a few months working in London, a vacancy came up for a secretary in Baghdad; and although only 19, she was chosen.

The brief of the Security Service did not normally cover foreign countries. But Iraq, like Egypt, was bound to Britain by past ties and by a current treaty under which there were British forces stationed in wholly British-run bases.

By 1950 the Foreign Office had started to fly its staff to foreign posts; the extra cost of air travel was outweighed by the savings in working days. But the armed forces continued to travel by sea with their equipment and luggage; since the Security Service was camouflaged as part of the War Office, their staff also travelled by sea. So Mary found herself booked on a troopship to Egypt.

Although telephones existed, international lines were poor
and unreliable; the telegram was the medium for emergency
communications, not for chat. Letters were the way to keep in
touch with relations and friends. During her two years away
Mary wrote 192 letters to her parents, many of them quite
long. What follows is only a small part of the correspondence,
omitting altogether mention of friends at home and details of
shopping and clothes, but I hope giving a fair idea of life and
loves in an expatriate society. I have changed the spelling of
some names so as to conform with current usage and to give
consistency; and I have corrected a few obvious errors such as
occur when writing a letter quickly; but I have retained most of
Mary's own punctuation. The letters are spattered with names
which must have bemused Mary's parents, who evidently
asked for details of the more eligible males while allowing the
remainder to wash over them.

★   ★   ★

CHAPTER 1

At Sea – Aboard SS *Empress of Australia*
01.04.50 - 11.04.50

At Sea – S.S. Empress of Australia   *1.4.50*

My darling Mummy & Daddy

…'Well, we had a very comfortable journey to Liverpool, enjoyed our sandwiches etc. We got in about 2.15, and I was greeted by megaphones blaring indistinct directions. However, with Col. Hoysted's help I eventually landed up in the right queue, did all the right things with my multitude of papers, and even more amazing arrived on board in the right cabin, with all the right luggage!!

…The cabin is *most* disappointing – we have got an inside one, and everyone else appears to have portholes and heaps of light. There are six of us (including one small child) crowded into about eight cubic feet, and it is extremely stuffy and noisy etc. But I gather that for a troopship we are in luxury! The other occupants consist of:- two R.A.F. wives going to Gibraltar, one of whom possesses quite a passable little girl, and the other two are *enormous* women – some sort of Mission Welfare W.V.S. stunt – I am a bit hazy. They are quite amusing, but incredibly hearty! One told me she liked 'the spirit of the cabin', and the other was delighted because she and I 'were sharing the same little corner!' I refrained from asking where my share was! I haven't really unpacked at all, as there is no room to move and it seems best to keep things in one's case. However, after Gib. the R.A.F. wives depart, so it ought to be better. I don't know what I should do without Col. Hoysted, as he has been marvellous. I have my meals with him and another colonel, which is nice'…

1

[same letter]   2.4.50

'Here we are half-way through the Bay of Biscay and I feel absolutely grand! After I stopped writing yesterday, a young officer brought me some tea and we got talking. I've found someone who knows Lloyd, and also seen Ronald Broughton, the boy who is engaged to Hope Richardson!! Isn't it amazing?!! We started playing liar dice after tea, and then they said they'd teach me bridge!! So we played bridge after dinner for a bit – I am beginning to get the hang of it. However, it soon relapsed into pontoon – and eventually that deteriorated into me giving advice on people's matrimonial problems!!! In one cabin there are six officers under 25 – one of which is married, three engaged, one free and one who doesn't know whether he's engaged or not!! Isn't it killing?! The one who I was giving advice to is a 2nd Lt. of 18 years who is engaged to a girl of the same age, and he is wondering whether she would consider coming out to Egypt. So I – feeling my $19^1/_2$ years, have been dissuading him, assisted by a very nice R.A.M.C. man of about 28!!

Oh! I am enjoying myself…

I meant to go to the early service this morning, but when one wakes it is impossible to know whether it is 12.00 at night or 7.00 in the morning. However I went to the big service at 10.30 with my three subalterns. We had the service in the main lounge, and it really was lovely. We had 'Eternal Father', 'There is a Green Hill', and 'When I Survey'. A nice army A.C.G. gave a wonderful and most impressive sermon. We ended up with 'God Save the King'. Then we went up on the boat deck and played quoits or something.

I am having a wonderful time, as several of these people thought I was a 'wife'!! Nearly all of the women are married, and there are a few W.R.N.S. etc., one brigadier's daughter and me! There is an awfully sweet wife called Mrs. Riley, who has joined us now and we are all going to play bridge again tonight…

I am having a bath tonight at 5.00, which will be very welcome'…

[Same letter]   *3.4.50*

'At the present moment I am writing this on the boat deck, perched in a rather precarious position. Every time the ship rolls I nearly slip off my seat. I am on the port side, facing the coast of Portugal…We are now opposite the most westerly point of Europe – Cape Roca – with a castle on the top which was the residence of the Portuguese. We can see the vegetation-studded cliffs lit up by a patch of sunlight which is shining through the overlying clouds (cirro-cumulus). (See what these stirring sights have done to my stilted style?!! Actually the last paragraph has been dictated by the R.A.M.C.!)'…

At sea – S.S. Empress of Australia   *4.4.50*

'I hope you've got my first letter, as it was posted in Gib…

There was a talk on the 'Empress of Australia' after tea, but I missed it because of post. However Col. Hoysted gave me a good resumé at dinner. It was built by the Germans in 1913, and handed over to us after the Great War as reparations. It was once a luxury liner taking only *120* passengers and today there are 3,500 on board!! It is the only ship of its kind to carry royalty twice in its lifetime – the 2nd time being when the Queen and King went to Canada in 1939. Apparently the King told the Capt. that he had never been on such a comfortable voyage. They had a cinema show in the saloon, just as we are going to, I think it is tomorrow. Isn't it funny to think of the King eating where we eat in the saloon? Apparently she is to be broken up at the end of 1950, so this will be one of her last voyages.

After dinner Mrs. Riley, Ian, Paul, Michael and I all had a go at horse racing. It is one of the standard amusements on board. There are six horses (wooden) and you back 1/- on whatever you fancy, and then they move them forward by shaking dice!! We did quite well to start with, but we gave it up when we got back to all square…

…when I got on deck the most wonderful sight met my eyes. We were steaming slowly into the harbour – on our starboard bow lay the Rock of Gibraltar itself looking simply magnificent. You could see the three peaks, the Lion Rock, all the houses and everything. On the other side stretched the coast of Spain – you could see the most lovely green fields and mountains behind. It really was a lovely sight in the early morning, with the calm blue sea and sun. On the other side of the bay you could just see the towering Atlas Mountains of Morocco. Isn't it thrilling?!!…We left Gib. At 10.00 and went round, and now we are well and truly in the Mediterranean. It is just like one is told and reads – boiling sun, blue sea, and cloudless sky!! I have just this minute seen my first porpoises, which are enormous black things looking rather like blunt sharks!

To my horror and fury we have got a woman with two horrid little girls in our cabin – isn't it sickening? It is even worse than before now. Actually it doesn't worry me when I am up in my bunk, as I sleep like a log now and don't feel the heat in the night'.

[Same letter]   *Wednesday*

'Today we are sailing about seven miles off the coast of N. Africa, and the long range of mountains along the coast is simply lovely…

Yesterday evening all the females were roped in for the Troops' Dance. I wore my taffeta frock, and it really was quite fun. It started about 8.00 and ended 10.30, so it wasn't too bad!! I was quite lucky, as I danced all the time with a *fearfully* superior individual who was doing his National Service!! He gave one the impression that he was at least the son of an Earl, and reminded me of J. Walker somewhat!! He lives at Honiton, knows the Sievewrights slightly – knows people I know at Harcombe House, and to top it all, has a flat in Drayton Gardens, so we found quite a lot in common! He was pretty ghastly though, and an appalling snob!! However we both won the standing statue dance, and I was given a voucher for 5/- to buy whatever I wanted at the ship's shop. I am very popular at the moment as I bought a set of poker dice! Col. Hoysted was horrified!'…

[*Same letter*]   *Thursday morning*

'This has got to be handed in tonight for posting in Malta tomorrow…

Yesterday I was roped in to play poker with four other officers – mercifully I did quite well – and kept my end up. We played for ages with each match being worth ½d!! But I ended up about all square, I think. They keep teasing me, and saying I am an excellent actress putting on an innocent act!! It is such fun – and it is amazing how much I've learnt already about men from being thrown together like this. Usually it has been the other way round! I am sure it is good for me!…

At Sea – S.S. Empress of Australia   *Good Friday 7.4.50*

We have just left Malta, where we arrived early this morning and stayed till about 2.00…

I am having a gorgeous time now, as thanks to Ronnie I have got into a very nice set!!…

In the evening I had a bath, and changed into my long frock, and then summoned all my courage to go and join the Brigadier's drink party. I then 'drinked' with an Admiral, a Colonel, a Group Captain and the Adjutant. No mean party!!! After dinner was *the* dance – and my goodness – it was TERRIFIC fun!! Unfortunately it ended at 10.30, but it was thrilling while it lasted!! I started off dancing with an awfully nice boy called Billy who went to Downside (one of Ronnie's lot!). He is an awfully good dancer, and we got on fine. Then the Adjutant (quite young) dashed up and talked to me and asked for a dance. Unfortunately I was booked. Then Col. Hoysted asked me for a dance and it was an 'Excuse Me'. It was lovely – I got no further than half-way round the room with one person – and I was whirled from Col. H. to Adjutant – to poker-game man – to R.A.M.C. – to Ronnie – to another awfully nice friend of his called Peter, and so it went on. The rest of the dance was hectic to a degree – and I couldn't remember who I was meant to be dancing with next!! It ended all too soon, and we adjourned to the lounge, where an almighty sing-song was going on. I had a rather unsuccessful attempt at smoking a cigarette, which caused terrific amusement, and resulted in my having a private lesson this morning on the boat deck!! Glen, – who undertook the instruction – says he will always remember me whenever he smokes – which is roughly 40 times a day!!...

A nice lady started talking to me this morning, and asked if I would mind being introduced to a Lt. who had asked if he could be introduced to me!!! Aren't I honoured?! So I had drinks with them at 12.30, and Peter (that's his name) was very nice. Who should join us but the *gorgeous* captain, who always smiles and peers at me round four rows of large bodies at meal-times!! So now I really have met everyone I want to!!'...

[Same letter]   *Saturday*

Only one more day of this life of luxury and 'reigning supreme!' [6d]★ I shall die of misery when this voyage is over – never have I had such a gorgeous time in all my life!! Last night the Adjutant winked at me three times during dinner [6d]★, and this morning the *gorgeous* captain talked to me for quite a time [6d]★. He has a father, a mother, a step-father, a step-mother, a half-brother and two half-sisters – so perhaps he's not so desirable after all! However he was very nice – and has just said that my 31/6d frock is pretty!!!

Last night we played tombola – a most terrifying gambling game that they always play on board ship. You have a card with rows of numbers on it, and they read out a series of numbers which, if you have them on the card, you cross off. The first person to have a full card wins some money. We formed a syndicate of about nine subalterns and me!! I was given the kitty to hold, as they wouldn't trust each other. We didn't win much, but the Adj. came and joined us, and when he won he gave us his winnings of 25/- which I have been taking charge of. I go round with a cigarette tin jangling hard!

I have been introduced to a John Collins – no – it's not a person, but a drink! Actually it was nice, and only tastes of lemon squash.

[Same letter}   *Easter Sunday*

'Just been to a very nice service at 10.30'…

We had horse-racing again, which really was terrific fun, as the gorgeous Captain, (who must be known hereafter as Michael Ibbetson(?)) made up and typed a real race card. All the names were very appropriate and terribly funny! The best

---

★See page 23 for an explanation of 6d.

was horse No. 3 in the Baghdad Stakes, which was called 'Baghdad by Girl out of Adventure!!!' Wasn't it clever?!!…I am afraid I lost the syndicate a lot of money last night, as of course we put heaps on 'Baghdad'. In that race the last horse in was the winner, and of course my wretched horse shot along and came in first! Maddening! Michael Ibbetson came up to me and said, 'Always rather fast, aren't you Baghdad!?' In the Maiden's Race we were all sold and I fetched 12/-!! Your poor daughter is not very valuable is she?!! However I didn't win again and I'm a rather expensive horse to keep!

We ended a hilarious evening of horse-racing about 10.30 p.m. and then we adjourned to the lounge!! We were all just settling down when the gorgeous Captain – alias Michael Ibbetson – said, 'would I come here a minute', so I followed him out, and he asked me to join a party in the Purser's cabin! I was frankly rather terrified, but I felt I could cope with it, so I went. There was the Adjutant and a WAAF girl, Michael and I, and then the Commandant and Purser etc. We all sat down and they offered us drinks. At this moment Commander Bilbow entered holding a cup of tea and a sandwich!!! Everyone laughed, (me rather enviously) and then he offered me a cup. I accepted, and jolly glad I did, as it settled the ginger ale and dash of whisky beautifully. He said that if ever you want to win a lady's heart, offer her a cup of tea after 10.30!! And quite true it is – I loved him for the rest of the evening. To counteract the tea I smoked a cigarette fairly creditably – thanks to my teachers!! We stayed there till about 11.30 and then the Adj. and Michael suggested we should go for a walk on deck! So off we trotted, and it was fun!! The gorgeous Captain (Cavalry) was quite amorous!! He said he'd peered at me at meals round various heads and said, 'Ah! My love from a distance!' He said I was pretty and attractive, and wore the right sort of clothes and ALL SORTS OF THINGS!! He also gave me fatherly(?) advice on life in Baghdad and said I mustn't marry in a hurry etc., etc. He was quite nice, though I should think about 30 or so!!

I will stop this now as the voyage ends at approximately 11.30 hours tomorrow. It has been a wonderful experience – and the most terrific fun! Perhaps it is just as well it's over now as I really *have* met everyone I wanted to now'...

★   ★   ★

CHAPTER 2

Fayid
11.04.50

Civilians' Mess, W.R.A.C. Camp, Fayid, M.E.L.F.17
Tuesday [11.4.50]

'I have been in Fayid for 24 hours now, and I never want such an experience again. I don't think I have ever felt so miserable or utterly desolated in all my life! I was snatched off the ship at 10.00 a.m. yesterday morning, and the awful thing is I haven't said goodbye or thanked Col. Hoysted. I don't know *what* he will think, as he had just gone off to find out who was meeting me, and when he came back he would have found me gone! I was one of the first to leave, and had no time to say goodbye to anyone hardly. Billy, Glen, Peter and co., I just managed to find in time – but no-one else. I left the ship in great style in a small launch with a Naval Commander from the office here!! Just as I was stepping in I heard someone yell out 'Goodbye Mary – and the best of luck'. That was my *gorgeous* Captain – I waved madly at everyone and really had a tremendous send-off!!!...

When I took my first look at Port Said from the boat in the morning the first thing I saw was a large advertisement for Johnny Walker whisky!! It is a funny place – as it is such a mixture of East and West. The streets are quite narrow and overhanging – just like the pictures one sees '...

We also went to the beach in the car and had a last look at the *Empress*. That just finished me – I howled and howled and howled. We then had an extremely snivelly lunch in a café on the roof, overlooking Port Said. Every now and then boat loads of troops from the *Empress* went past and dissolved me once again!'...

We got to Fayid about late tea-time, and there another awful shock awaited me. It is just one large camp and nothing else – at least it is several hundred camps all looking exactly the same. We are in the W.R.A.C. Camp (all women!) which is a large compound surrounded by barbed wire (9 ft. high) consisting of hundreds of stone huts. We have our own rooms in one of these huts, and eat in a mess which is especially for civilian women. I was put in my room and left to unpack. My goodness – it is a small square room – stone floor – vaguely distempered walls – black iron bed – iron table – cupboard – chest of drawers and a cracked mirror. On the bed was a grey army blanket, and over the windows there is small-mesh netting, and outside that there are large sort of criss-cross bars – really it couldn't look more like a prison cell if it tried!!...

About 11.00 the naval chap collected me and took me to the office to fill in various things about my passage. They have put in for an air passage next Tuesday now, so I shall have at least a week here'...

I was taken down to the Egyptian Police Station this morning to hand in papers. It was rather interesting as we had to go through the Arab village. There were real mud huts and people carrying water pots on their heads and everything!! Gosh – the filth and squalor though is unbelievable'...

I am beginning to cheer up a bit now, as although Baghdad is so far away, I think it will be far more civilized than here...Of course, the whole trouble with me is that I am thoroughly and desperately boat-sick!! There I was the only eligible female – everywhere I went people stared – and I was always surrounded by men – and except for night, I never spoke to a woman all day long hardly. This is a terrible contrast! I don't think I have ever been so happy as I was on that ship. It got better and better towards the end too!'...

Fayid   *13 April 1950*

'I am settling down here now and recovering from my boat-sickness, though it still gives me a pain to think I shan't walk into the lounge and see all those familiar faces. I still yearn for John Collinses, and my smoking lessons on the boat deck etc. etc.

This afternoon I met several people from the boat, as being a half-day, we went down to the Officers' Club to spend the afternoon and have tea. The Club is right on the edge of the lake and has its own beach, and is really very nice indeed. I went down with one or two other girls, but unfortunately I couldn't bathe as it looked simply lovely in! There I saw the Padre from the ship, and then saw a group of subalterns who I vaguely remembered, but hadn't spoken to. Luckily they remembered me and one of them came over and we had a terrific talk. They were all sent to Kabrit first, and have only just got settled. They had seen my friends and gave me all the 'gen' about them, which was nice...

I am dreading tomorrow as I have got to work for Major Franklin (who is acting head of S.I.M.E.) as his secretary left today. It is awful just taking over for a couple of days, and I shall probably make an awful hash of it!...

The Mess is very comfortable. There is a dining-room with little tables of four – a lounge and a sort of front bit with comfortable chairs – and a bar. The meals are really excellent, and beautifully served. We have three courses for lunch and dinner, and an enormous breakfast if we want. They bring us early morning tea to our rooms at 6.15 a.m. and also afternoon tea if we want. The batmen are awfully good and make our beds, clean shoes, and keep the place clean. It really is comfortable in that way!!'

The Security Service had its regional headquarters with the Middle East Land and Air Force Headquarters at Fayid. The Head of S.I.M.E., with whom Mary had lunch, was Brigadier Bill Magan. Baghdad was an outstation; the establishment while Mary was there was two officers, two secretaries and one registry girl. The secretaries could double up for the registry girl if she was away, but the registry girl could not do shorthand. Philip Ray was Mary's chief for her whole tour; Kenneth Hornby and Roger Lees were successively his deputy. The three girls lived together in a female staff house, and since they figure largely in Mary's letters, I list them here. It was Isabel Body who was the other secretary during most of Mary's time; she was eventually succeeded by Mary Frankland. The senior secretary was at first Janet Marshall; she was followed by Pauline Pascoe who did registry work only; and when Pauline married she was replaced by Elizabeth Burt.

The Air Officer Commanding (Iraq) lived at Habbaniya, but he had a house reserved for himself and his guests in Baghdad, known as 'Air Lodge', in charge of a Sqn. Ldr. who also did liaison duties with the British Embassy and really had quite an idle life. The Security Service Office in Baghdad was located at Air Lodge, and camouflaged as 'A.H.Q. Detachment'; later it moved into and became part of the British Embassy.

★   ★   ★

CHAPTER 3

Baghdad
17.04.50 - 14.08.50

A.H.Q. Detachment, R.A.F. Baghdad, M.E.A.F. 19
Monday 17 April, 1950

'Baghdad at last! And *what* an agreeable surprise I got after all the fearsome things I'd heard and after Fayid too! It is *enormous* and has real houses, streets, cinemas, street-lighting, shops and heaps of other things. I honestly never expected anything more than a large straggling group of mud huts! It really is far more civilized than I'd ever dared to hope – why we even have lavatories with chains to *PULL*!! I'd almost forgotten how to pull a chain!

But – this won't do, I must go back and start at the beginning as here is HEAPS of news to tell you…

I worked quite hard at the office while in Fayid, but it got me back in practice which was a good thing!… On Friday, Major Franklin, who I had been working for, asked me to lunch with his wife, which was very nice of them. They live in one of these 'Family Villages' and you all eat communally in a mess. It is all very nicely done – but rather grim really for families. We had a very nice lunch anyway, and I met the Senior Padre off the boat and his family!…

I had just heard that morning that I was flying on Sunday instead of Tuesday, so I had to get cracking. I worked again in the evening, and was introduced to Mr Magan – Head of S.I.M.E. He had just arrived back from one of his tours, but wanted to see me. He is awfully nice, and they all worship him

14

at Fayid. He talked to me, and warned me not to eat this and that in Baghdad, and was most helpful. Then he asked me to lunch on Saturday to meet his wife. They have self-contained quarters in the 'Family Village' which I find *far* nicer, as they have their own servants and meals served in their house…

On Saturday…I went into Ismailia with Mrs Franklin and another officer in the car. Ismailia (where Col. Hoysted is) is about 20 miles up the canal on the way to Port Said. It is quite a large town – very dirty – but quite good for shopping…Then we went to a café called Antoinette's and had a cup of coffee. There I saw a real life FIRE-EATER!! He came along and performed outside for our benefit!! He put flaming things into his mouth, and then drank benzine and shot flames *out* of his mouth, and finally leapt through a flaming hoop! But – rather thrilling wasn't it?…

I summoned up my courage and decided I'd brave the Officers' Club by myself, hoping I'd find one of the other girls down there. I got a bus down, and just as I was stepping into the entrance of the club, who should be standing there but Ian Wallace!! (The boat one of course!). We fell into each other's arms (metaphorically!) and talked nineteen to the dozen…Joey (Ian's friend) asked if I'd like to come down to the Club in the evening and dance. I thought I was rather silly saying 'yes', especially as I'd got to get up at 5.00 a.m. to get the plane – but still I was determined to say I'd danced in Egypt – so I agreed…We walked in, and there at a table in the corner were the nice R.A.F. types from the boat and the W.A.A.F. who had come to the Purser's party!! It was just too good to be true, as they were awfully nice…We had a wonderful evening – just like old school gossip – Apparently the R.T.R. (Tanks – Peter, Glen and co.) are very near Fayid, so it was a shame I didn't see them. Michael Ibbetson – the gorgeous Captain, is in Fayid till 8th May and also the Adjutant. I almost felt I wanted to stay in Fayid – but I'm *terribly* glad I'm not there now. I don't think any

of those Canal Zone places are very thrilling – nothing but
huts. Although you probably have a gay time there, I should
think you'd get far more bored than out here…I eventually
persuaded (with difficulty) Joey to take me back about
midnight, so that I wasn't *too* late. He was really very nice, but a
bit too amorous for first acquaintance – one worse than our
friend Bob Clark!…

…by 7.30 a.m. I was stepping into my first aeroplane. It was
a Valetta – fairly small, but very nice inside. It was lined so that
the noise wasn't too terrific. It was really only carrying freight,
but there was one other passenger besides me – a very nice
Flight Lieutenant. It was great fun, as they (the crew etc.) knew
it was my first flight and were awfully nice! The 'Captain' was
an absolute *poppet*, and I fell for him on sight. He was small and
fair and looked about 19, but actually he must have been about
25 as he was an 'A' pilot which is very rare! So I was in safe
hands you see.

Well, I sat with the nice Fl/Lt., who told me *everything* and
explained every *sound* practically. First of all the engines revved
up, and then we taxied along for miles, and then suddenly we
went very fast for a few yards and then suddenly the ground
was miles away. It is incredibly quick, and you hardly know
you've left the ground. Once we were up I felt safe again – but
just before we started I thought my last hour had come.

When we were up we could loosen our safety belts and walk
about or do what you please. Oh! Joy! – they had a lavatory in
the tail, I was so relieved. It was an Elsan, so my little theory of
it going straight out into the air must be wrong. I am so glad,
aren't you?!

…We went over Amman, which is a very large town, and
where King Abdullah lives, and on to Mafraq where we came
down. Once we were up in the air again I started feeling sick. I
think it was probably because there were lots of air-pockets –
and we kept bumping up and down. I snoozed and tried not to

feel sick for a bit, and then one of the crew came along and asked if I would like to go forward. So along I staggered and sat right in the front of the cockpit with the pilot!! They are dual-controlled you see, so everything opposite me was exactly identical to his. The noise was deafening, I wore earplugs for a bit, but even then I couldn't hear a word the poor man was saying. I discarded them and he showed me things by pointing etc. Then he made me *FLY* the wretched aeroplane – I had to steer by keeping a line horizontal on another line and by keeping something else at 9,000 and watching about six other dials. Still – although we flew at varying angles – it was a terrific experience. Not many people fly their plane the first time they fly – *and* across the desert!! I stayed in front until we got in sight of Habbaniya and then went back to my seat – still feeling desperately sick!! We circled round Habb and the Fl/Lt. had just said only five more minutes when I was sick!! Wasn't it terrible?! It was literally just as we were coming down too. Luckily we had cardboard cartons of sandwiches, and the Fl/Lt. *just* had time to tip out everything, and we *just* saved my dress! Poor man – what an awful companion to have on an air trip – I can't think what he must have thought'…

★   ★   ★

At this point it may be worth sketching some background on the Iraq into which Mary stepped in 1950.

Modern Iraq was created after the First World War from the three Ottoman vilayats or provinces of Basra, Baghdad and Mosul. There is some geographic sense in creating a separate state out of the basin of the Tigris and Euphrates rivers, though its inhabitants did not then and do not now form a homogeneous nation. In 1950 the total population was some 4,500,000. Most were Arabic speaking, though the 800,000 Kurds were separate racially as well as linguistically. Sunni Moslems formed the elite in the centre and south, but there were some 2,000,000 Shi'is whose holy places of Kerbala, Najaf and Kadhimain were to be found on the Mesopotamian plain. There were some 100,000 Christians of several denominations; 100,000 Jews who were supposed to have been there since the Captivity in Babylon; Yezidis, who take the view that since God is good, he will not do you any harm, but that the devil being bad should be placated by worship; and Sabaeans or Subbi who worship John the Baptist and need to live by a river so as to practise their daily immersion. The Christians included Assyrians and Armenians who had fled from the massacres in Turkey after the First World War and had been accepted by the British as refugees. All had of course been treated by the Turks as minorities under Ottoman rule; and they continued to live side by side but with little social intermingling under the Mandate.

The British Mandate had been imposed on these peoples by the peace settlement; the Arabs feeling that they had been cheated of their independence by the victorious British and French. The British for their part felt some guilt about their promises to the Hashemites of the Hejaz, and imposed on Iraq a constitutional monarchy under King Feisal, one of the leaders of the Arab revolt against the Turks. The Mandate was ended in 1932, when Iraq became notionally independent; but a 1930 Anglo-Iraqi Treaty constituted a military alliance under which two British air bases were retained on Iraqi territory.

The Mandate was not originally very welcome to the inhabitants of Iraq, but the advantages of Pax Britannica over the arbitrary despotism of the Ottoman Turks was soon appreciated by the mass of the population, and it was only in the second half of the 20th century that Arab or Iraqi nationalism became much of a force. During the Second World War there was a brief revolt in favour of the Germans, but immediately afterwards British influence and friendship was fully restored. In 1950 King Feisal II was at school at Harrow, and his uncle Abdul Illah was Regent. Parliamentary democracy had never taken good root, and in the 1950's there was a series of rather weak governments; Iraq's only real statesman was Nuri Said, who retained the confidence of the Royal Family. It was widely believed that the real fount of government was the British Embassy; though in practice the British had little desire to exercise political influence. But British influence and power was very apparent in other fields. The airbase at Habbaniya, 60 miles from Baghdad, was large and well-manned. Most banks and important foreign trading companies were British-owned and run. The Iraq Petroleum Company was British-run though internationally-owned. British technical assistance in such fields as irrigation and aviation was paramount. There was a British expatriate community in Baghdad of maybe 1,000. English was of course the main language of education and commerce.

Social life was free and easy. The different communities worked together without much friction or discrimination, though at play they tended to keep to themselves. Law and order prevailed; as a young girl of 19, Mary was able to walk alone around the city of Baghdad and take public transport with no more qualms than at home in England. Most unattached young expatriates lived in single-sex messes or shared suburban bungalows; that way they could afford a fair degree of comfort, with perhaps a cook and a houseboy. Social life centred on clubs; the Alwiyah Club was the main British-run club, and had sporting facilities as well as dining room, lounges, bar and a few bedrooms; while there were establishments such as the Railway Club catering for employees of all nationalities of Iraq State Railways and its subsidiary Iraqi Airways.

★　　★　　★

[same letter   *17 April 1950]*

'As we stopped I saw a large fat man, a large fat lady and a tall thin man with a camera. I guessed they were my people, and they were. I dismounted (is that the correct term?!) from the plane in great style, and was greeted by a string of christian names. However, I sorted them out later in the day and discovered that Sqn. Ldr. Seear (large and fat) and Fl. Lt. Tweedie (tall, thin) are in the liaison office at Habb and vaguely connected with our office. (By the way we work as R.A.F. out here – that is our cover for all purposes!). The fat lady is Janet Marshall – the other secretary – who is leaving for U.K. in about a month. She is nearly 50, but quite a nice old soul. She rules our staff house – can't think how Isabel and I will get on alone!…We didn't bother about lunch as I'd just been sick, and just sat in the club at Habb and rested. We had a nice tea and then went for a stroll. It is a lovely place – a real oasis – green trees – lovely gardens and everything. We went for a walk through the Command Gardens (R.A.F.) which are quite a showpiece – and really are lovely. There was the most heavenly smell of honeysuckle everywhere, which was like a breath of heaven after the 'wog' smells of Egypt! The whole place is a large R.A.F. Centre – but very nicely planned with permanent buildings. You can stay at the club for the weekend and they have Saturday night dances for the R.A.F. officers etc. So I must get down there sometimes – it is nice to feel there is a place like that to go to, even if it is 60 miles away. There are lovely swimming pools, tennis courts etc. too…about 7.00 p.m. we started our homeward journey…It was a heavenly drive over the desert at that time in the evening, as it was just dusk. The desert looked all mysterious and heavenly, and smelt simply lovely – I don't quite know why! We saw heaps of Arabs in flowing headdresses, but unfortunately they were usually riding motor-bikes or donkeys – but never dashing across the desert on snow-white Arab steeds! Just outside Habb there is a signpost put up by the R.A.F. saying:

BAGHDAD	LONDON
60 miles	3,500

or something like that!! We crossed the Euphrates at a place called Falluja, and it looked heavenly with the palm trees reflected in the water and all the lights etc. The approach to Baghdad is lovely too, as you see the lights simply miles away. The Tigris is magnificent and looked lovely last night. I really think the moonlight was the best time to enter Baghdad, as it really was most impressive. We went past the Regent's palace and saw King Feisal's in the distance. We passed the airport and the station and the Syrian Gate which is rather a fine piece of architecture. We then seemed to go for miles through brightly-lit streets. It really did look *thrilling* and I am looking forward to exploring. Our house is in the residential part – quite a way from the shops. The office is five miles from here – right the other side of Baghdad – so you can see what a large place it is.

As we drove up to the house a whole fleet of servants was lined up outside to welcome me!! Oh! What a pleasant surprise the house was! It really is lovely. It is built of brick with a flat roof where we all sleep in the summer, and has a tiny garden. As you go in the drawing room is on the left – a lovely light room with two windows, sofa, two armchairs, wireless, bookcase, standard lamps etc…Then through glass doors is the dining-room, with a nice polished table. Isabel's room is on the ground floor and also the bathroom, hall, lavatory and a sort of odd room where we wash and there is a fridge and a store-cupboard etc. Then you go up the stairs and my room is on the right and Janet's on the left. I think mine is the best of the lot as it is large and cool. One window faces N.W., (which is apparently *the* thing as I get the prevailing wind) and the other S.W. There is a door onto the balcony so I can get quite a draught when I rest in the hot weather. I have got a large very comfy divan bed, and *two* wardrobes, a chest of drawers, a dressing table, a long mirror and a chair – all in green paint. It looks nice and fresh anyway, and I have put the Lane's chair up as it matches and makes an 'easy' chair! I have been given two little bowls of roses by one of the servants – so with my Easter cards it really looks quite gay!! Then I shall buy pictures in due course and mats for the dressing-table and so on. But it really is luxury after Fayid and so fresh and clean. The whole place has character and I am sure I shall love it…

Thanks awfully for your cable, and also for your letter Daddy which I got this morning. Yes – Mr Roberts is the Padre here and Isabel and I are going to join the choir!! She said she would if I would, so I said I'd come and be a 'body' anyway! It might be rather fun! Tomorrow I work – we work 7.30 to 1.30 Monday to Saturday and then we are finished for the day, which is nice. But we only get a *fortnight's* holiday a year. Still – three months when I get home'…

Baghdad   *23 April 1950*

Philip Ray is my 'boss' and head of the office out here!! I have met Bridget his wife, as they asked Isabel and me to tea at their house last Wednesday. So we met the children and everything. They seem very nice but Philip is mad keen on work and his family and that is literally all. He doesn't appear to take any interest in anything else, and according to Isabel couldn't care less whether we lived or died! I must say he certainly does give that impression – and I haven't taken to him exactly. Kenneth Hornby – the No. 2 – is quite different – cheerful sort of chap and quite willing to help anyone.

…I have survived one week of work anyway, and it doesn't seem too arduous. This week I have been picking up the secretarial work – one of them keeps shooting in and asking me to take down…They dictate terribly fast, and the names are terrible to learn! However, I think I am getting on alright, and it is nice to have so much shorthand again! Next week I am going to learn the registry work, filing and finances – so that if one goes on leave I shall know how to cope! Janet Marshall, the older secretary, leaves in three weeks and Isabel and I are being left to cope! It is quite a responsible position really, as now they are only sending a girl from Head Office for the Registry, and we are to be left in sole charge!! I gather Mr Ray didn't really want me in the first place, as he has had a run of bad luck ending up with a young girl (19) who had to be sent home as she was such a hypochondriac, so I shall have to be *awfully* good or I shall get sent home, I expect!!…

I meant to explain the [6d] in my letter [of 7.4.50] – but quite forgot!! It was on board you see – our syndicate of Billy, Peter, Glen and Co. and me had a little scheme whereby if any of them talked 'shop', or I mentioned my Colonels (of whom they were secretly very jealous!) or any of us made an indiscreet remark of any sort, we coughed up 6d into the kitty as a fine! My goodness – it kept our kitty going strong, as one hardly had to open one's mouth before 6d dropped out!! After I'd gone to bed they used to play pontoon in their cabin, and continue the forfeit system down there, because every morning I was handed a weighty tin of the previous night's 'fines'!! Also, if any one of them took an unfair advantage of the other and took me off alone round the boat deck – they forfeited at least 5/-. They *were* funny!…

…I am a member of the Alwiyah Club now, though I haven't paid my subscription yet. I am all fixed up with an account at the British Bank of Iran and the Middle East, which is nice – and have changed my money etc. and had my photo taken for passports and what-have-you.

On Tuesday I went and had a swim at the club. It is a lovely pool – nice and clean etc. After dinner Isabel and I went back to the club for play-reading, which they have once a fortnight; we did 'This Happy Breed' – which was quite fun. I have had two good games of tennis…They have hard courts, and we have *dear* little Iraqi ball-boys!! You pay 1/- a go for tennis and about 9d for swimming, so it's really not very cheap!…

I've actually seen an orange growing on a tree! Isn't it thrilling? But guess what they cost? About $5^{1}/2$d per *orange*!! On the way to work we pass a mosque and there are often storks on the top of it!!…

Yesterday evening – at least this morning – I wasn't in bed

until 3.15 a.m.! – it was the St George's Society dinner and dance. I am now a member of the Royal Society of St George!! It was a really *big* occasion, and I was quite awed. I had to wear my blue taffeta again, as my trunks still haven't come. Pat Tweedie from Habb and a Sqn. Ldr. called Derek Ford who works in our office were our partners. We had drinks here first and then went to the Alwiyah Club for the dinner. My dear – it was *terrific*! Huge long tables – we all had our places named – and beautifully printed menus (which were flown out from England). We had a real English dinner – Severn salmon (also flown out!), roast beef, Yorkshire pudding and apple pie etc.! We had to drink whisky for all the toasts (filthy muck!). We had a toast to our King, King Feisal, and heaps of other people. Then they read out cables and messages – and there was one from Buckingham Palace!! Then we had after-dinner speeches. The first was by an Englishman proposing a toast to our guests (the Irish, Scots and Welsh). Then the respective 'nationalities' replied. They were very amusing of course – but the best speech of all was by a Welshman. He really was brilliant – and absolutely brought the house down! I laughed and laughed!! Dinner started at 9.00 p.m. and we finally started dancing at 12.00!! The Ambassador and Mrs Mack were there – and I didn't think much of her – especially as she wore a *short* dress! The Air Vice-Marshal and Mrs Air Vice-Marshal were also there and several other big-wigs – so it was all very entertaining. I danced with Pat quite a lot. He is Scots and awfully sweet…

Today I slept till 10.00 a.m. and then Derek Ford took Isabel and I to the races at Al Mansur, just outside Baghdad. It was wizard as we were guests of the Secretary and had a sort of box in the stand! The *awful* thing was you couldn't put on less than 5/- a go – so having lost 10/- I didn't bet any more! However, it was fun and I've learnt the Arabic figures if nothing else – as all the numbers were in Arabic. Oh! The Regent of Iraq was there, and when we were in the Steward's part we were *frightfully* close to him. He looks rather nice. He keeps his wife in Purdah though – which is a pity as she is supposed to be lovely. The little King wasn't there today, as he had gone out to tea! We drifted around – feeling very royal – and it was quite an experience! Thank goodness we just made church as I was feeling guilty!'…

Baghdad   *28 April 1950*

'Isabel and I went to our first choir practice on Wednesday, holding each other's hands in terror. The Padre was very pleased to see us – at least he was at the beginning, but I wouldn't like to say at the end! I sat next to a very nice Dutch lady, married to an Englishman, and she had a marvellous voice. I piped away beside her, hardly even hearing myself – however afterwards she remarked on what a nice voice I had!! I said the suitable remarks – and she said it was no compliment – but the truth! So obviously, at last I am inheriting my father's beautiful tenor voice…

Isabel Body is an *extraordinarily* nice person, and I really feel safe with her. Her father is quite a famous doctor, I gather, and also they are very rich, but real gentlepeople of the old type. Her father is about your age and sounds very amusing (like you) and has the same outlook on life. She has been awfully well brought up, and always knows what is right and wrong in etiquette, and what one should wear on such and such an occasion – which is all most helpful to me. She also knows who one should avoid and that sort of thing. We were in alone last night and had a terrific talk about everyone and everything, which was most interesting. Actually she said, that as foreign stations go, Baghdad is an exceptionally nice place from the moral point of view, and that there are really hardly any 'wolves' in Baghdad. I must say all the people I have met so far are exceptionally nice, and not even superficial…

I am simply loving it in Baghdad – and this week has flown…

I have just joined the British Institute with Isabel, as I think it is another GOOD THING. It is only 30/- a year – and it is a sort of junior branch of the British Council. Its aim is to foster friendly relations with the Iraqis, and actually there are very few British members – so we both thought it would be most interesting to join. They have concerts, excursions, lectures, and bridge parties and all sorts of things. We went along there on Wednesday night and played bridge. I had at least five Iraqis all teaching me wrong – so I got on fine! Last night we went along as the Head of it (a very nice Englishman) was giving a lecture on Wordsworth. It was awfully interesting, and stirred my brain slightly, as it has been lying dormant since Higher! The Head promised to find someone to teach me Arabic cheaply – as Isabel's teacher charges 10/- a lesson! I couldn't afford that, but I feel I must learn it. I think it is awful to live somewhere for two years and make no effort either to learn the language or get to know the people. That is another reason why I have joined the Institute, as it gives one other interests than just hanging around the Alwiyah Club!'…

Baghdad   *Saturday 29 April, 1950*

'…We went to the Ray's party about 8.00 and I wore my new frock – which really *did* look gorgeous, although I says it as shouldn't. It is a lovely frock and fits beautifully. Well – we had drinks on the lawn for literally *hours* (while I supped lime juice) and talked. Mr Magan was there, as he had been staying with the Rays, also Oscar Seear and Pat Tweedie – the two R.A.F. types who work in our Habbaniya Office – Derek Ford – Kenneth Hornby and his mother (our second boss) – a young married couple I didn't know – Sammy Lloyd, another R.A.F. type from Habb., and a Captain Jimmy Butts in the 'Devons'.

He is a most extraordinary young man and it was rather funny as Isabel had told me heaps about him! He looks about 40 – but according to Isabel is only 24! I just *can't* believe it, as he looks terribly old! Isabel had told me how *terribly* slow and dull he is at talking – and of course as luck would have it, I got saddled next door to him! We had a wonderful buffet supper – all sorts of odd dishes. One was pineapple rings with cheese on top, which is apparently a Canadian dish. We also had 'pilau' which is a sort of national dish out east, consisting of rice, raisins and banana (!) and heaps of other things!! It was all very good anyway, but we sat out in the garden till after 12.00 p.m., and my bites irritated *so* much I nearly went mad. Jimmy Butts said, 'Would I like to see the night-life of Baghdad?' So I hedged in my normal feeble fashion till I could discover what the others were doing. Janet and Sammy were going to go, so I said I would, thinking Pat and Isabel etc. would be coming too. However, poor old Pat is still suffering from gyppy tummy and backed out. So just Jimmy, Sammy, Janet and I went along. I was rather apprehensive, but it turned out better than I'd expected and was really quite good fun! We went to a night-club called the 'Abdullah' (so I've been to a night-club at last, although it isn't quite the same style as the Coconut Grove – I'm sure!!). It was rather reminiscent of a village hall – the band was on the platform, and a dance floor in front – then tables and chairs all round with a bar at the back. We walked in and the first person we saw was our little RAF clerk from the Office!! All sorts go – high and low – Iraqi, British, and I should think every nationality under the sun!! We danced quite a bit, and Jimmy Butts was really quite interesting and not at *all* bad. He told me a lot about Beirut which I have been thinking of for my leave! After a bit we joined up with Col. Bird's party – and they suggested we should move on to 'Ici Paris' – another night club!! However, 'Ici Paris' is on top of the 'Abdullah', so we only had to climb a few stairs!! That was a tiny place, with fearfully dim lights, chairs etc., and a floor the size of a 1d stamp. They all have wonderful cabarets of French dancing girls, I gather, but we were too late for that last night! A chap called Brian Foxmale was up there too, and I had met him at the races last Sunday! We were introduced, however, again, and I said that we had met at the races! However, Brian replied with great vigour, 'Oh! Yes, of course, we met at the *MASONS'S*'!! So I left it at that!! Later in the evening we were introduced yet a third time and he said, 'Ah! Yes, we have met *many* times!' Well – we stayed there till about 3.30 a.m. and then went in search of food. We eventually came to a *dreadful* little place that is open all night, where we had a truly Arab meal of kebabs (meat sausages roasted on a stick), all sorts of pickly things, some *awful* stuff, humoussa – sort of goat's cheese or something. I didn't eat much as I'm still breaking my stomach in gently, and it looked like poison to me!! However, I am o.k. this morning, though I don't know why!!'…

Baghdad　　　　　　　　　　　　　　　　　　　　　　*6 May, 1950*

'…Isabel gave a cocktail party for Janet, and we had it here in the house with about *50* guests!! It was a roaring success…I met heaps and heaps of new people, and really feel I'm getting to know people now. It *was* such fun, as Oscar (from Habb) and Janet were both trying to introduce me to two *gorgeous* young men at once!! The one from Habb. Is a Major Bestley – quite young and quiet and nice-looking. The other is the new British Vice-Consul, Archie Rendall, who has been out here about a week longer than me! Janet met him at the Embassy party, and asked him along especially to meet me as she thought he was so nice!! He is a Scot, and *fearfully* young to be a Vice-Consul. I should say he's about 25 or so – but then I can never tell. He was terribly nice anyway, and we talked hard for ages!! Janet was sure I'd made a hit – but I don't think so, especially as we saw him later in the evening at the Abdullah with a girlfriend!!…Who else did I meet? Oh! Yes – a dashing young individual called Philip Mallet, another Embassy staff. I was really quite cheered by the end of the evening to think there could be so many young people in Baghdad – especially after the morbid stories I'd heard!!…Most of the people drifted away about 9.00 p.m., but Kenneth Hornby, Jimmy, Derek, Col. Bird and Sammy all stayed on for *hours* just sitting/drinking and talking. Eventually about 11.30 p.m. they suggested going off to the Abdullah to see the cabaret. I wasn't going but eventually gave in for peace and quiet and thoroughly enjoyed myself. The cabaret was terrific – real-life kan-kan girls in red net stockings and frilly panties doing high-kicks!! It was fun, and also various dancing girls doing wonderful handstands and backbends! Everyone sat drinking and getting tighter and tighter, so Isabel and I insisted on being brought home about 2.00 a.m. I woke moderately easily at 6.15 a.m. to discover that Janet had come back about 3.00 a.m. plus Sammy who was in no fit state to go home. So Janet slept in the hall, and Sammy in her bed. (Baghdad life!)…

'…I paid my first visit to the bazaar (or 'suq' as it is called here) and it really was thrilling. You walk along endless passages lined with stalls, filled with the most thrilling things. You could literally spend *hours* there. We walked out through the Coppersmith's Bazaar which is the most colourful of all. Everyone bangs away at their bit of copper – making the most terrific din. We had quite a day of 'local colour' as on our way to the Institute, Isabel and I took our lives in our hands and took an 'arabana'! They are horse-drawn cabs of the most ramshackle appearance imaginable. Europeans *very* rarely use them, although they are far cheaper than taxis, but I expect they are bug-infested!

'…Oh! Jimmy Butts has asked me down to Habb. Next weekend…'

Baghdad   *11 May 1950*

'...You say you want to hear what I eat – well, here goes:- for breakfast we have orange juice, and then Janet and I have some stuff called LEBEN which is almost identical with Pa's Bulac! It is sour milk and is very good for gyppy tummy. Then we have a boiled egg, toast and marmalade. (All very English – except for leben). Then for lunch and dinner we have ordinary muttons, beefs, etc., plenty of vegetables, beans, peas and potatoes, and ordinary English sweets. Then, of course, if one goes out to an Iraqi restaurant (like the one we did after the Abdullah!) you get proper Iraqi food such as kebabs, masquf etc. etc. We have a cook called Bakr who is a Persian Kurd, but speaks quite good English. The 'boy' is the same nationality, but speaks no English. They are very honest, but of course you have to keep on at them to sweep under the bed etc! I have just succeeded in getting my bed swept under for the first time since I arrived. According to Kenneth they will only do it once a month!! Still, I think they are just *so* marvellous, and can hardly believe they won't walk out next minute!

My daily routine is this:- woken by thumps and yells from Janet at 6.30 a.m.; stagger down to breakfast about 6.50 – wild rush ensues – and frantic hooting, which is Philip [Ray] at the gate. We all dash out forgetting to bring our 'faces', and flop into the car. Then we have a nice sleepy drive – and I am awoken again on reaching Air Lodge! We work happily away till about 8.50 a.m. (the mail to Embassy leaves at 9.00 a.m.!). Kenneth then suddenly dictates three or four letters all to go to Embassy – another wild rush. After Embassy mail has safely gone we flop again, and have to be revived at 10.00 a.m. by a cup of chai (tea). (Oh! Blessed hour – 10.00 a.m.). Then things go fairly calmly after that, gradually culminating to a climax at 1.15 p.m. We leave the office at 1.30 p.m. and get home for lunch – faint and starving – about 2.00 p.m. After lunch we all drift our separate ways. I usually wash, mend, iron or rest or write letters and generally do my odd jobs. We have tea any time between 4.00 and 5.00 and if nothing is happening I usually go down to the Club for swimming...

...I have been to Babylon – seen the ruins and 'by the waters of Babylon we sat down and' – ate!! Last Sunday morning Kenneth sent me a note asking me to fill a gap in the car as his mother couldn't go – so I had a lovely outing to Babylon. It was a lovely run – about 50 miles or so – and then we got there. There is a small museum, where one parks the car etc. and collects the Arab guide. Then we set off round the ruins – it is absolutely thrilling and you feel you are walking on countless generations of famous people. It is on three levels – and the Germans excavated it in such a way that you can see all three at different spots. The Ishtar Gate, which is at the entrance to Procession Street – leading to Nebuchadnezzar's Palace, is visible, and we walked along Procession Street. On the walls there are animals carved, which stand out in relief...We also saw the Lion's Den, which is supposed to be Daniel's, but I'm not sure about that...We then saw where the Hanging Gardens had been – and the various foundations of Nebuchadnezzar's Palace. There is an enormous lion carved out of stone, which the Germans couldn't remove, so that it is there still...There were odd bits of stone lying about with Cuneiform writing on it – and it was all most thrilling. Of course, really we only saw over the site of the actual Palace and immediate surroundings, and the Inner and Outer Walls of the City were miles away on the horizon!...We had lunch by the Nil Canal, which is just near the Euphrates. Then we drove round and I took a couple of photos. There were some buffalo coming down to water, and their herdsman, when he saw me, instead of fleeing from the evil eye of the camera, posed against one of the buffalos!! He made me laugh so much I missed getting him in the end!! The people there weren't very used to

Europeans, and all the children crowded round to watch us go!
I also saw a Moslem praying to the prophet on the way home.
It really was a great experience. Now I must read up about
Babylon before I go again'.

Baghdad   *15 May 1950*

    '...Well, I have just had the most heavenly weekend down at
Habb. Jimmy Butts came up on Saturday in his car and took
both Janet and me down on the Saturday afternoon. We had a
very pleasant drive except that the road was full of puddles and
every now and again we received the most tremendous shower-
bath! We arrived for tea at the Club, and joined up with
Sammy, Pat and Oscar and the nice Embassy girls...We all went
and changed and eventually met in the A.H.Q. Mess at 7.30 for
an enormous drinks session...We eventually went to the
Officers' Club for dinner at about 10.30 p.m.! We had lots of
tables pushed together, so we were all at one large table. We had
a stupendous dinner, hors d'oeuvres, soup, chicken, sweet,
coffee, sherry with the soup and buckets of champagne! They
have got a huge roulette table in the Club, so we adjourned in
there for a bit after dinner...Then we danced a lot off and on
till 3.30 a.m. I thoroughly enjoyed it, as for once we danced
nearly all the time, and duly came back to the bar for a drink
between dances. I loathe it when we get settled down at a table
with drink, as no-one ever feels inclined to get up and dance. I
danced with Butts quite a lot, but it was quite a free and easy
affair, and I had one or two with complete strangers. A very tall
fellow came along and danced with me quite a bit too. I
subsequently discovered his name to be Perry Fellowes, and I
thought he was quite nice, but Janet says he is unpopular with
the others. (However, I don't count on that as her friends are
more than slightly peculiar!). But he is quite harmless which is
something! Anyway he says he is coming up to Baghdad in a

fortnight with some others, and wants me to come out to dinner and on to dance or something later, which would be great fun!…

The next morning I came to and pottered over to breakfast at about 9.00 a.m. It was the most gorgeous sunny morning and I lazed over my breakfast, of fruit juice, scrambled eggs, toast and coffee! Then I read for a bit and eventually everyone rolled up and we spent the morning by the swimming pool. I bathed about three times, and sunbathed the rest of the time. I have got beautifully burnt, and I hope it is going to turn brown in time! Jimmy didn't surface until about 1.00 p.m. and nor did Pat! We dressed and went to the bar for drinks before lunch, and eventually settled down to the traditional curry lunch at about 2.45 p.m. After that Jimmy, Ursula and I went for a walk through the Command Gardens, and then right out along the Euphrates river bank. We had decided to stay at Habb. as long as possible, so as no-one else was coming back to Baghdad we had to share a taxi. It was only 35/- for the whole way back to Baghdad at 11.00 p.m. which didn't work out too badly divided amongst five. We went to the cinema at Habb, in the evening and saw an awfully good film called *Marry Me*. It was a J. Arthur Rank and most amusing! The cinema was open air, which I imagined would entail a flapping sheet for a screen, but not a bit of it! I quite forgot I wasn't inside in the middle. We eventually left Habb. About 10.00 p.m. and got back to Baghdad at about 12.00 OH! and wasn't I tired this morning!…

I really did love my weekend, but I don't like Jimmy much. At least he is so *odd*. He is so slow it isn't true when he does talk, which isn't often…!'

Baghdad   *21 May 1950*

'…I met Bill Startup – the nice man who takes Isabel and I to early service. He was having trouble with his car, but eventually he got it going and said he'd run me home. We went on out to look at the floods on the outskirts of the town. Apparently it is an annual event these tremendous floods, but this year they are terribly late and no-one was expecting them. There are bunds (which are high banks) all round the town, but someone breached it, and the water poured through sweeping away hundreds of mud houses. There is a terrific stretch of flood land – and whole streets and rows of brick houses are half-submerged. Luckily we are out of the danger zone, but I gather it has done a lot of damage to crops as well…

On Friday night we went to Bill Tidman's party. It was very exclusive – mostly Iraqis and very few English…I was stuck beside a fabulously wealthy sheikh who, in one breath, asked me to go racing with him, offered to teach me riding, offered to teach me Arabic if I taught him English, and so on. Once again Mr Gueritz came to my rescue!…

You know I told you about the persistent Iraqi who has been ringing up the Gueritzes trying to get them to arrange a meeting? Well – we at last have had to tell him that I am engaged to someone in England!! (I wonder who the lucky man is!). So, all is well now. But I *do* have to be so careful!'…

Baghdad   *25 May 1950*

'…I am in the midst of an absolute whirl of gaiety at the moment…The Embassy girls' cocktail party on Tuesday was great fun. We…Moved over to the Havana for the rest of the evening! The 'Havana' is a very nice night-club, especially as it is outside now, which makes it far less sordid looking…I met an awfully nice young man called Capt. Neville Dowding – he is an Iraqi Airways pilot – English of course, and is a friend of Johnny Forder. He was gorgeous – quiet – and apparently not one of the terrific party-goers!…

…I went on my round of the banks the other morning, and

in the Eastern Bank the Manager – John Norman – saw me and asked me into his office. So I sat in comfort while my money was being collected. At the Iran and Middle East I paid Arnold Crow a visit and was given two peppermints. I am getting the hang of the work now, but I shall be relieved when my first end of monthly accounts are done!…

…It has been lovely and warm out here – the other day it was *108* degrees in the shade. Just imagine it? Actually it was quite nice, and I calmly proceeded to do my washing, ironing and mending during the heat of the afternoon. I dripped incessantly, and drank great draughts of water, but I felt fine. I think I shall survive the heat, if I don't go crazy and play tennis or something in the heat of the afternoon, and I shall try to sleep in the afternoon too. The worst thing is the BITES – they really are chronic. Mine are *slightly* better now, but my arms look as though I have had very bad measles. Last night at Air Lodge the mosquitoes were appalling – and it was rather funny to see very smart ladies wearing hats and stockings etc. balancing on one leg, while kicking out wildly with the other, not to mention balancing a drink and cigarette in their hands while talking to the Ambassador or Lady Mack (Needless to say the only lady without stockings was Lady Mack!). I didn't think much of her, and worst of all she and Mrs Boothman (the Mrs A.O.C.) fight like cats in public, which is rather poor in the two leading English ladies…'

Baghdad   *28 May 1950*

'…On Thursday I met Perry Fellowes for lunch at the Alwiyah Club – we had a drink first and then an excellent lunch. In fact we didn't finish till about 3.30 p.m.! He is 32, almost a Squadron-Leader in the Iraq Levies. The Iraq Levies is composed mostly of Iraqis with British Officers seconded from the R.A.F. Regiment, and is really more of an army than air force, as their purpose is to guard the R.A.F. Station. He is quite nice – but I'm not smitten in the very slightest! We went on to the races for a short while – and I lost ¹/₂ dinar as usual. But it was quite fun...

On Friday...We went up to this cocktail party and dinner dance which was really rather dull. Isabel went home with Jack Sallis to hear records, and I stayed having arranged with a dreadful young man called Gordon Bell to give me a lift home. However we were just going when we were asked by the Chief of Ceremonies at the Royal Bilat to stay and have dinner. So we had to stay, as he is one of the highest of the Iraqis and the Regent's right hand man!!! So we stayed to have a 'little light supper' which consisted of five solid courses, not to mention wine from Chateau Mazarin (one of the very best makes I believe!). I also met his son who is the Chargé d'Affaires in Switzerland, and a Syrian Minister. They were all very charming indeed, and really very nice. (Far preferable to the old sheikhs anyway!). Tahsin [Qadri] – that's his name – is a Pasha – and I had to call him 'Excellency'! He showed us over the Regent's Pavilion at the Race Course too. The killing thing was when his son turned to Gordon and I and said, 'Have you any children?' I was speechless – but Gordon said, 'No – we hadn't – in a very off-hand sort of way – adding *hours* later that we weren't married!! It *was* funny!'...

Baghdad   *31 May 1950*

'...I simply must tell you about Denis Shepherd, who I told you I met at the A.O.C.'s cocktail party. He was at the Sworders' party on Tuesday – the Test Pilot party – and we had a long talk. I had heard from Isabel that he is supposed to be one of the nicest people in Baghdad, and I am sure it is true. If only there were lots of *unengaged* Denis Shepherds in Baghdad it would be an excellent place. Anyway he has restored my faith in man, and inspired me to remain as I am. (The latter is a great thing, don't you agree?). The Ambassador was not at the party, so he was fairly free, and talked to me a greater part of the time. I don't really know why – but I suppose he recognised a kindred spirit or something…He told me that he found he drank less and less alcohol out here as time went on, which is the first time I've heard anyone say that! He also told me it was all rot when people told me to drink whisky etc. as it is so good for you. He asked how I liked it (Baghdad!) and how I liked the people etc. We agreed everyone was very pleasant but of course they were all exactly alike with a few exceptions! He said that there were some very nice people, but the majority are rather boring – just whisky drinkers etc. However he was quite nice about them. He is going home soon, and I don't know whether he will be coming back with the Ambassador or not. I don't expect so. He really is quite one of the *nicest* men I have ever met – and as Mary F. and I would say, '*Wholesome*'…

…Isabel and I are blossoming out as entertainers now, and we are having a dinner party tonight, followed by going to the cinema at the Club…are coming…and Philip Mallet…Philip Mallet is the commercial secretary at the Embassy, and obviously will be an Ambassador one day, as his father is His Britannic Majesty's Ambassador to Rome!…He is extremely nice – very young and I believe very clever. I think it ought to be a good party anyway…'

The Test Pilot party was another large do, with, I should think, all the mosquitoes in Baghdad invited too. There was the usual agony of balancing drink, eats, cigarette in one hand while kicking out madly with free arm and both legs!…Archie Rendall, the Vice-Consul, cornered me for a good bit of the time, so I really thoroughly enjoyed myself!

Isabel and I and Mr Ray all went to tea with Kenneth and 'Mum'. It was very pleasant and most amusing…I was telling Isabel she *must* get married out here as it was my life's ambition to be a bridesmaid. Philip [Ray] said he would see to it that I could be a bridesmaid before I go home. We got on to the subject of marriage and I was informed that of the previous lot of Embassy girls three out of four had got engaged or married while out here – 75% as Kenneth said!! Another man was telling me that if you only came out for two years – you don't get married. His idea was that during the first year you flit about – and during the second you may meet someone – but that you are home before you know where you are!! So I hope that is what will happen to me – I have no wish to get married out here at all!!'

Baghdad   *5 June 1950*

'I'm feeling very Monday-morningish at the moment. I have just started sleeping out on the roof. I slept out for the first time on Saturday night, and it really does make a tremendous difference. It is lovely and cool getting into bed, and even the sheets feel cool, which they never do in the house. I have got an iron bed, which is extremely comfortable, with a large mosquito net over it. It is lovely lying looking up at the stars – and it is so cool I even had a blanket on last night. The worst part is the morning, because although the sun doesn't wake me too early, it is terribly hot even at 6.00 a.m.! So I think I shall get some sort of shade put up, then I will be fine. Last night some sort of mosquito must have got under my net, as I have got two lovely bumps on my forehead!

'…Saturday – Oh! Great joy! I have been asked to the Caledonian Society dance!!…I am going with Archie Rendall – the Vice-Consul!! The other morning our R.A.F. clerk was away, so I had to take the mail over to the Embassy. I had just deposited it, when I bumped into Archie, who swept me away to his beautifully air-conditioned office for a cup of tea! Actually it was rather lucky as I happened to have my passport on me and so I was registered there and then as a British Resident, with the official stamps. No-one had ever told me I was supposed to register at the Embassy, so if it hadn't been for Archie I suppose I shouldn't be entitled to British protection or something! Anyway I had a very nice cup of tea in his office, and he said that he had been meaning to ask me for ages to the Caledonian Dance and would I come! I am so thrilled, as he is awfully nice…

I have just had a most exhausting weekend. Perry Fellowes came up from Habb. With some dreadful people called Wing-Commander and Mrs Newbury and a F/Lt. Goldsmith…We all had dinner at Air Lodge…I foresaw a rather dull party, as the Newburys are the most dreadful couple. She has got ash-blonde hair, and says she was Lady-in-Waiting to the Princess Royal – poor Princess Royal!…We danced a bit and then went on to the Havana…we went on dancing – and W/Cdr Newbury kept trying to make me dance the 'night-club' way – all efforts which were strongly resisted by me! (I met Gordon at the Club yesterday morning and he had witnessed my efforts and advised me to buy a pair of knuckle-dusters!)…I danced with Perry quite a lot, but he is far too serious for me. I shall have to choke him off firmly from now on! It was really rather a dreadful evening and they were all (except for Perry) incredibly vulgar – I think its funny up to a certain point – but they really were the end. However, they all raved about me apparently, and thought I was so wonderful, pretty, etc. etc., until I was nearly sick! I got Perry to take me home eventually and left them to it…

What a nuisance men are! Why can't they all be like Denis Shepherd, gorgeous captains, Billys, Lloyds and Michaels! Still, it's all EXPERIENCE – and *frightfully* good for me. I am slowly learning to 'differentiate'. Anyway don't you worry about me. My old head is becoming firmer and firmer screwed on!…

We had slight excitement the other morning as the body of a

murdered woman was washed up on the shore at the bottom of Air Lodge garden here. Poor old Derek had to go and look at it, and as it was of some few days murdered, the smell was appalling. The other day just before choir practice the Padre had to deal with a riot in the cemetery. Apparently we had bought some land to enlarge the cemetery and the workers were down there with knives quarrelling about it!'…

Baghdad   *11 June 1950*

'…I had the most wonderful time possible last night at the Caledonian Dance!! It was such a refreshing change after the Abdullah and Havana etc! I have fallen completely for Archie Rendall – I never knew he was so *gorgeous*!! (Yes – yet another joined that happy band!). I am dreadful – I fall for almost every other person!!! (Still – only young once!!)…I had played tennis in the afternoon and yet for some reason I wasn't a bit tired the whole evening and didn't even have my customary sleepy time from 11.00 to 1.00 a.m.!! I managed to talk a lot and was even quite amusing at times. I find I get on *far* better when Isabel isn't there as she gives me a slight inferiority complex!! (Poor ugly daughter). We did heaps of reels – the Eightsome, Strip the Willow, the Dashing White Sergeant and something else. Anyway they were all ones I knew quite well which was lovely. Mercifully it was an exceptionally cool evening with a very cool breeze, but even then we got *terribly* hot and our throats went dry in an awfully funny way. Everyone was giving the most feeble croaks for 'Hoicks'!!…We had ordinary dancing in between, and I danced with Archie all the time, except for one with Mr Edwards. He is *terribly* nice (Archie I mean!) and he has got my sort of sense of humour (rather feeble – you know). However we got on *very* well – at least I hope so. He has got a lovely smile and went to Fettes. (Is that the school in Edinburgh, or do I mean Loretto?). His dog is having puppies and he has offered me one. But I must see them first before I decide!...It was a lovely evening, and *so* different from last Saturday with those dreadful Newburys!!

Last Wednesday, as I told you, Isabel and I went to dinner with Kenneth. Ralph Watts – one of the Iraqi Airways seconded pilots – was there to make up the numbers...Of course Ralph Watts (yes – I expect you can guess!) is quite exceptionally gorgeous. He is tall and *BLONDE* – my undoing! He is a wonderful pilot and also very clever, I believe. However I should imagine he's a bit conceited, although he was very pleasant. I had a few heart throbs for him, but they've been replaced by A.R.!'

Baghdad   *16 June 1950*

'...On Tuesday Bill Startup took Isabel and I for a most interesting drive round the town after tea. He described and pointed out everything, so I learnt quite a lot. We went over the other side of the river through a very poor and old part of the town known as the Karkh area. It was very dirty, but awfully interesting. We then went on to Kadhimain – which is a suburb a little way out. That is where the very sacred Mosque is, and no Christians are allowed anywhere near it even. Kadhimain is the 'Mecca' of the Shi'is (local Moslems) and no Christians are allowed to live there at all. The Mosque is the most wonderful building with four gold minarets which are lit up at night, and in the day you can see them glinting in the sun. There is $^1/_{16}$" of real gold leaf on them. After leaving Kadhimain we came back to Baghdad over the Bridge of Boats, which I'd heard about from Mr Drury. It is lovely – and if you get heavy traffic going over, it bounces up and down. The boats are moored facing upstream and then there is a wooden road laid from bank to bank over the top, and quite heavy traffic goes over it. We came into the north end of the town, and saw the Royal

Mausoleum where King Faisal and King Ghazi are buried. We also saw quite a lot of interesting buildings, and the remains of the old wall of Baghdad which was blown up by the Turks in 1917. We also saw all the floods, which *still* stretched for miles and miles…

On Wednesday night we, at last, went out to the Royal Armoured School (Iraqi) at Abu Ghraib and had a Masquf dinner with Colonel Basri. The Padre and Derek Ford were there too, but otherwise it was all Iraqis. We sat round in a large circle on the lawn and drank and talked from about 8.30 to 10.30 before we had dinner. It is supposed to be rude to serve the dinner early, as in Iraq they always leave as soon as they have eaten! So we sat there talking for hours. I talked to an Iraqi Colonel who had been to Larkhill on a course, and also knew Salisbury. On my other side there was an awfully sweet Iraqi girl who didn't speak much English – but she was awfully sweet. The Colonel, who is a Moslem, was telling me all about the Holy Month of Ramadan which started yesterday with the new moon. From sunrise to sunset the Moslems fast and are not supposed to eat, drink or smoke during that time. It must be dreadful not even being able to drink in this weather. Some of the *very* strict ones do not even swallow their own saliva – but I gather they are very few and far between. Of course, as always, it isn't very strictly kept by the upper classes – and it is the coolies who stick so rigidly to it, when all day they are running up and down Rashid Street with grand pianos on their backs. Ramadan changes each year, and is getting earlier and earlier at the moment. We had the most *enormous* meal, and I felt ill for the next two days!! I sat next to an Iraqi lawyer who kept loading up my plate as fast as I made a small indentation!! We had masquf, pilau, and heaps and heaps of etc.'s (luckily it was too dark to see what I was eating so I just swallowed and hoped for the best). After that we had fruit, and I was rather staggered when Mrs(?) Basri, the hostess, came up to me with her plate of fruit and popped something into my mouth with her spoon!! But that too, I gather, is a *great* mark of honour! After the meal I was surrounded by an admiring crowd of Iraqi females which quite overwhelmed me!! I discovered the nice girl who had been sitting next to me had two equally sweet sisters and a (not so sweet!) brother (the lawyer). Anyway they insisted I should sit with them, and they asked me to visit them. So, remembering the Padre's words, I accepted an invitation to tea last Thursday. They live right out in N. Baghdad so I had to arrange to be collected by the brother, and taken there in the car'…

The next day, Thursday,…Zaki – the lawyer collected me from Orosdi-Back's at 7.00 p.m. He took me to their house and all the girls were waiting. I gather their mother and father are dead, as they have a much older sister who keeps house for them all. The three girls are all about 18-28 and are at the Higher Teachers' Training College and know Miss Oliver. Anyway I was most royally entertained. We had a terrific tea with masses of cakes and terribly rich buns and heaps of fruit! (All extremely bad for my already weakened 'tum'!!). The tea was *quite* extraordinary but apparently I shouldn't have put milk in it!! It was like hot Horlicks or something. Their house was very nice – and nothing particularly un-English about it – except that it was rather large. They told me all about their meal-times etc., and also taught me a little Arabic. I can now say, 'please', 'thank you', 'good morning' and 'good evening' which is really useful. They really were sweet girls and they gave me two silver brooches made in Iraq and also – a *wonderful* present – a picture all framed and everything. The middle sister does art, and she had lots of paintings done by her friends and she absolutely *insisted* on me having one. So I have got a picture in my room at last!! It is a painting of a bit of the river – and really very good. Their style of painting is very English. Zaki brought me home about 9.00 with many requests from the girls to come again. The brother is going to teach me Arabic, starting next week. To my great relief Pat Godfrey wants to learn too, and I am going to suggest he takes us together as I *didn't* particularly want to learn alone with him...

...Yesterday...after tennis...I sat and talked to the Evans! When Archie had changed, he pottered over and joined us, and also Isabel, Philip Mallet and finally Pat. We all had a drink and talked for ages. Philip Mallet really is one of the most amusing people I've ever seen, he had me in fits the whole evening. He has bought (in the bazaar!!) the most amazing old two-seater [Chevrolet] – which he says, 'goes like a bomb'! We entrusted our lives to it, and were shot, bumped, and jolted home!! There is a back-seat, but no leg-room at all, so Isabel sat lengthways on it – Mummy fashion! It is most dangerous as the steering wheel has 2 ft. of free play before anything begins to happen!'...

Baghdad   *20 June 1950*

'...After church on Sunday night we were collected from the Club and taken to this Masquf party, which was given by Sheikh Mohamed Ali as a farewell to Bill Tidman. I wasn't looking forward to it a bit, but actually it was a lovely party and I enjoyed it far more than the last one. There were quite a few English there, so it was about half and half...It was given in this Sheikh's 'Town House', quite near where we live, so we didn't have far to go. Another time he is going to ask us out to his real home in the desert, which will be much more fun. Then you recline on couches during the meal (Roman fashion) and don't have any knives and forks. He was a terribly nice Sheikh – one of the few really good types – and not a bit like Sheikh Ghazi!! This man is very pro-British and is one of the stalwarts of the British Council. We all sat round in his garden having drinks first, and they had a gramophone going

on the verandah so we danced a bit. I danced the samba with
the Sheikh – and he could do it jolly well – in fact his style of
dancing was exactly like Michael's, so I was quite at home and
we got on fine. He didn't seem at all hampered by his long
robes! I can't think where they learn to dance! (I bet not many
girls have danced a samba with a real life Sheikh in all his
tribal robes!)…

You remember I said I was going to learn Arabic with a
certain Zaki Karim? Well, I thought at the time that the name
sounded vaguely familiar – and yesterday morning I came upon
it – so to speak! (Comprenez-vous?!). I tore into Mr Ray in a
panic, and he was terribly nice and roared with laughter, and
said I must play the old Eastern game and slide out of it as best
I could with countless excuses! So I rang up yesterday and said
I had decided not to do Arabic after all, as I was taking up
French instead, and wouldn't have the time!! So now I am
hoping for the best, but I expect I shall have to go to their
house at least once more, as it looks rather rude. However, all is
well now and Pat Godfrey is going to learn Arabic with me
when we can find a suitable person. What a life!'…

Baghdad   *26 June 1950*

'Philip [Mallet]…asked us both to the cinema on Thursday.
We wondered whether he would bring another man to make
up the party, and when he arrived on Thursday evening to
collect us – who should the fourth be but Archie!! So
everything was *gorgeous*!!! They both came in and had a drink
with us first – and then of course Philip found he had left his
wallet behind!! Pandemonium reigned – especially as Archie
had just been telling us he never carried more than two or
three dinars loose on him!! However they refused our offer of
assistance, and scrambled through the evening somehow – with
frantic writing of cheques, chitties etc.!!…The film…'This

Time For Keeps' – was an appalling American musical. However we four thoroughly enjoyed it, and roared with laughter in all the wrong places!! We danced afterwards for a short time…I had several with Philip, who really is most amusing and terribly nice. I had the last with Archie – who is *quite gorgeous*!! So it really was a perfect evening!! I wish you could have seen us careering home in Philip's two-seater. Philip, Isabel and I were somehow wedged into the front, while Archie crouched on the seat (that isn't) with his knees up to his chin!!…

It was such a contrast with Saturday's party at John Moore's which I *loathed*…The party went on till about 3.00, by which time John Moore – the one host – was completely speechless with sleep and drink – and the other host had disappeared to take his girlfriend home!! (Neither of them *ever* asked me for a dance!). Not that I wanted to dance with either – but I thought it was bad! Isabel was there in another party, and they left just before us. As she went she came over to Kenneth and said, 'would he see me home' which I thought odd! However after offers of a taxi from Perry – we all (mercifully) piled into John's car and were driven home at a reckless and breakneck speed. I was in the back with Perry, Ken and American girl. When we dropped the girl, Perry *would* put his arms around me – *revolting* – but I wasn't having any. When I was dropped at the house, to my joy, Isabel was still up – and had had a dreadful party too. So we had a *wonderful* gossip about all the dreadful people there are about. She then told me why she'd asked Kenneth to take me home, as she'd been learning dreadful stories about Perry. Jack Sallis had told her that it wasn't safe to let me go home alone with him, as he was looking for a WOMAN TO SLEEP WITH!! (Phew! That was a narrow squeak. Actually as he was spending the night with J. Moore I don't quite see how it would have worked!). Also, apparently, there is a rumour he was or is married to a cabaret artiste who ran away and left him (sensible woman!). So that's the end of me and Mr P.F. for good and all!!'…

Baghdad   *30 June 1950*

'…On Monday…Arnold Crow took us both to the British Institute to hear Mozart…Archie Rendall (the light of my life at the present moment) was there too. So I begged a cigarette (to keep off insects) off him in the interval, and we had a nice talk, and I even managed to be quite amusing for a change. He was *terribly* nice and kept smiling at me etc. So I thought perhaps I'd made a hit – but TRAGEDY hit me the next day as I saw him leaving the Club with another GIRL – my heart is broken – however, I feel fine on it – so perhaps he is not the light of my life after all!!!…

P.S. I haven't drunk alcohol for *ages*. Luckily I can always plead thirst in this weather and have a squash. Nor do I smoke'.

Baghdad   *2 July 1950*

'…I went to a wizard cocktail party last night and drank 'white ladies' and champagne cocktails!! It was simply wonder-ful as I was really quite amusing and terribly talkative – quite a change for me, and for once I didn't feel dull!!…

…I am so glad you think Archie sounds nice. I have com-pletely lost my heart – but *awful* things have been happening – and he is getting very friendly with a girl of 25 called Sue Cotton. (One of the Embassy girls – but *not* our lot – you know – not quite such a nice type). My heart is broken – and I don't know what to do, as she is nice to look at, but there isn't much in her – you know the type. I suppose I must just plod on as I am and hope for the best. Any motherly advice?…

Tomorrow…In the evening, Isabel and I are going to the

American Independence Day party with the two organists…! Very dull and proper…Oh dear – I am undone! I bet Archie will be there with Sue Cotton too!! Meaow!!…

Much love from your love-sick daughter, Mary.

(P.S. Not really!!)'

Baghdad   *16 July 1950*

'I am sitting being 'Reception Committee' for Pauline Pascoe who is expected to arrive about 11.00 p.m. from Habb. Tonight (yawn! yawn!). Isabel is out, so I promised to be in. I have had great fun putting finishing touches to her room, last minute dusting etc., putting out of towels, and after tea I found a few roses and popped them in a vase in her room. I think it makes such a difference, don't you?…

Well, I've been to two stunning parties this week! Max Reynold's on Thursday, was one of the best I've been to out here. To start with he lives in the most sumptuous house possible, as it is used as the I[raq] P[etroleum] C[ompany] guest house. There are air conditioners in every room, a stair carpet, wonderful furniture and – best of all – a mosquito-free garden!!…There were about 24 people there and all terribly nice…I was introduced to a new man at the Embassy called Nigel Power, who is *terribly* nice!!!!…Prepare yourself – its coming again!! He is simply GORGEOUS!!!! He danced with me a terrific lot, and is an ex-Gunner and knows Larkhill, *loves* Salisbury and is Registry Clerical Officer at the Embassy. He said he was in the army for the last two years of the war, so I should think he is about 25or so. (More later). He left the party early, and said nice things about not wishing to leave me!!!

Saturday…night was Gordon's farewell party, and Mr Ray took us with Nigel!!! That too was a jolly good party, though beginning to get rather drunken by the time we four left at 2.30 a.m.! I danced heaps with Hamish, and also with Nigel. He really is terribly nice – a serious type – but not too serious!! I should think that he has a better character than Archie (pity!) and really is most mature in outlook. Isabel thinks he's about 30, but I don't think he's as old as that! Anyway, he is another 'good, wholesome' type and not a Perry. He ranks with the Archies'! He was at the pool again today, and they gave me a lift home. I wonder if he is going to replace Archie!!…

Much later 12.40 a.m.!! Miss Pascoe arrived and we dragged in Philip [Ray] and Nigel(!!) for a drink. She seems frightfully nice…We had a gay little party – and I chatted alternately to Pauline and Nigel! He is simply *GORGEOUS* – it is no good – I've fallen again!!!…'

Baghdad   *24 July 1950*

'Life is wonderful, superb and gorgeous once again and I am feeling full of the joys of spring etc. etc. It just shows what a day at Habbaniya does for one!! Yesterday was one of those perfect days when everything goes 'according to plan' don't you know?! I woke on the dot of 6.00 a.m. (quite unheard of!) feeling fresh as a daisy (even more unheard of!) and got dressed etc. and Bill picked me up at 6.30 a.m. and we went to the Early Service. It was a lovely morning and a lovely service. The Padre was very pleased to see us as there was only one other person in the congregation!…I pottered about getting ready till 10.30 a.m. when Johnny Forder (Iraqi Airways pilot) came to collect me. I wore my nice new yellow frock that I got at Fenwicks – remember? Then loaded up with swimming things and a bottle of water for the journey we set off. I sat in the back and Ursula in the front…My goodness – it was hot on the way down! There was a terrific sort of hot wind blowing off the desert that parched your skin in a second! I got the worst of it as I was in the back and nearly blown away! We stopped once for a drink and then pressed on. However it was comparatively

comfortable and we arrived in Habb. about 12.45 which is
pretty good in such a small car. When I got up off the seat of
the car, there was a terrific wet patch – which was perspiration
and not what you think it was!! But wasn't it dreadful? It just
shows how hot it was. We literally fell into the pool
immediately on arriving, and it was quite empty, as everyone
else had gone off for the 'lunch time session'. It is such a
heavenly pool, and yesterday they had all the fountains round
the edge playing, so that it was like swimming in the rain.
Goodness, I have never been so ready for a swim! When we
had recovered we went over to the Officers' Club and were
hailed from the lounge by a great crowd of people – including
Kenneth, Pat Tweedie and heaps of others. So we joined them
and I drank *two* enormous pint tankards of lemonade straight
off!! I then consumed about a pint of tomato juice, and was
really 'coming to' at last!! We eventually all moved into lunch
about 3.00 p.m. and all sat at one large table. I met Mr Perry
Fellowes on the way, and we exchanged a few non-committal
remarks! Heaps of people were down from Baghdad because of
the cricket match…We had an excellent curry lunch followed
by fruit and coffee and eventually rose about 4.00 p.m.! When
we got up we had all stuck to our chairs with the heat, and I
had a sopping patch on my seat (my own!) which luckily didn't
show terribly. But one girl there had on a pale mauve frock and
when she got up there was a soaking patch on her dress at the
back, which looked dreadful, but there is nothing one can do!
After lunch it was too late to think about having a rest as the
cricket started at 4.30, so Pat, Ursula and I just fell into the
pool again, had a cup of tea about 5.00, and then pottered over
to watch the cricket. For once it was really exciting and quite
the most thrilling match I have ever watched. On the Saturday
the Casuals (Baghdad) had been all out for 83, and yesterday
Habb. went into bat, very confident that they would beat such
a paltry score. However when we got over there the score was

68 for 7 – and the tension was terrific. Oscar, who is the captain and rather a good bat, was out for two – unheard of – and consequently wasn't in the best of tempers! It got terribly exciting and Habb. really did look like winning when it was about 79 for 8. However, Johnny suddenly bowled number 9 out, and there was only one left to go in. The score got up to *82* and the tension was immense. I thought we hadn't a hope. They played one very careful over with Gundry-White bowling and no runs scored. Then with only two runs to win the match, Johnny bowled and got the middle stump first go!! We all cheered like mad as it is the first time the Casuals have ever beaten the R.A.F. Station! Hare, the Captain, was terribly excited…We all went back and had another drink on the lawn and then I left with Hare about 7.20. It was lovely going out to Habb again as it is a nice change and so restful…Even going back in the dark there was still this hot wind!! Gosh it was strong too, and my hair was everywhere. It was a simply wonderful car, one of the new 1950 Humber Imperials – large and spacious and beautifully sprung. Inside were ashtrays and little switches and gadgets – it really was lovely. We simply whizzed home at about 65 or 70 the whole way – imagine it! The result was that we were back in Baghdad by twenty minutes to nine which was just perfect for me! They very kindly took me straight to Jack's…Well, I arrived looking like I know not what. I just poked my nose round the drawing-room door, saw Archie looking rather staggered, so hastily withdrew it again. Pauline had very kindly brought my seersucker dress along so I had a good wash and changed and tore a comb through my locks, put on my best 'face', and braved the company! The Swiss Consul and his wife were there, Archie, Isabel, Pauline and myself. It was the most gorgeous evening and I really have quite fallen for Archie…He really is terribly nice, and I have found out lots more about him. He was in the Navy all through the war from the beginning, and is going to

be *29* next month! *Terribly* old! He lives in Edinburgh, likes music, art and reading. He arrived in Baghdad exactly one week before I did, and he thinks the time has *flown* too. The party finally broke up about 1.00 a.m., (not through any fault of mine who was frantically trying to prolong things, having been up for 18 hours at a stretch). However, Jack took us all home and Archie (who lives in the opposite direction) had to go off all by himself in the station wagon. I lamented this point!

Pauline is extremely nice and terribly efficient, but only nicely so. She is reorganising everything in house and office but it really is a good thing as things are in a dreadful state, especially the house. I never liked to do much about the house as Isabel was more or less boss there, so I just left it. However, Pauline is marvellous and the sort of person who worries over a thing until it is done. Apart from being efficient, she is very nice as a person and will be extremely good for me (i.e. she tells me to keep my stomach in and all that sort of thing!). I gather that she was engaged and that he was killed quite recently, and she took this job to sort of break right away. I feel very sorry for her, as I don't think she likes the place at all, but she is very plucky about it…'

Baghdad   *31 July 1950*

'On Saturday…we played a very nice friendly game of tennis. I played with Philip [Mallet] and we pretended to be Drobny and 'Gorgeous Gussie' Moran!! We beat the others hollow but it was great fun. Philip really is terribly nice and so jolly funny. About halfway through the second set he said, 'Let's have some champagne'. I thought he was joking but he asked the boy to bring it. However the boy must have been of the same opinion as he brought the usual glasses of water!! When we'd finished tennis, Philip again insisted on champagne and explained that it was his sister's wedding day! So we changed and then sat on the lawn and drank champagne to Lady Dunboyne – who at that moment was driving her new husband on a honeymoon to Ireland, having only just got her [driving] licence a few days before the wedding. I gather he can't drive at all! Poor Philip said he was feeling dreadfully old, as his sister is only 21! She was married at Wittersham (?) Kent…

Kenneth's party was terrific!…At about 1.30 a.m. the 'phone went, and it was one of the Embassy girls in an awful panic as their house was on fire. Apparently their 'fridge had exploded and caught fire, so immediately half our party dashed gallantly to the rescue!! After an hour or so they arrived back full of beans, though rather grubby about the trouser legs. It was most amusing, as I think only about one of them had been much good!! Max Reynolds took it upon himself to go into all the bedrooms and see if the mattresses were alright 'as they are inflammable'. He came back with a full description of how many wore pyjamas and how many nighties!! However it was got under control quite easily and no harm done…

…I am jolly glad I went to church as the Padre preached an excellent sermon, and most appropriate. It was all about how easy it is in a place like this to neglect the cultural side of life, and the things that are really worth doing, and to pay too much attention to the parties and other really unimportant things. I am *determined* I shall not just think of parties, as I am much happier doing the more worthwhile things anyway…'

Baghdad   *3 August 1950*

'…I wish I could make up my mind which I like best out of Nigel and Archie. Isabel gets terribly worried, and says that really I can't fall for everyone (Oh! Can't I?) and I must decide which I like best. I fail to see any reason why I should do any such thing. A much better idea would be to wait and see if *either* of them like me in the very slightest? There – isn't that good sound common sense for you! Decide which I like best indeed, the very idea of it. Actually I think perhaps Nigel has the nicer character, also he goes to church, and according to Isabel will go 'further' than Archie!! But – Archie's smile…'

Baghdad   *7 August 1950*

'…Jane Mitchell and Kenneth Clarke are engaged!!!…Isn't it a thrill?! They are both so happy – it isn't true…

Pauline…Is terribly nice – and awfully good to me. I feel quite safe with someone 'behind me' so to speak, now. We were talking about Jane Mitchell, and getting married in general yesterday – really a terribly interesting conversation – Pauline says that in her experience it is the girls who are always natural, and above all, easy go get on with, that get married more than the very pretty ones. I got rather worried as I am sure I'm not 'easy to get on with', but Pauline says I am, and that when I'm there she knows everything will be alright and quite natural and pleasant. It was very nice of her to say so, but I'm not sure I'm not at all easy – as I always feel awkward etc. Still – who knows – perhaps I have some hope after all! She has bet me a dinar I shall either be engaged or thinking about it by the time I go home in two years. So that's two bets now – Colonel Body's that I won't be engaged by my 21st – which I shall certainly win…'

Baghdad   *10 August 1950*

'Ain't life just FUN?!!! I am nearly off my head with excitement for a million and one reasons. To start with I have no work to do and am just bouncing with superfluous energy…

Life is never dull in Baghdad, I can assure you. We are in the midst (Isabel and myself) of being O.C. Entertainment for Test Pilots!! I have learnt more about jet Attacker planes and aeroplanes in general this week than in all the rest of my life put together. I am even getting rather interested in aeroplanes (and the pilots!). But, to start at the very beginning – Jack Sallis, as you know, is the agent for Vickers Armstrong out here and so he has to look after all these pilots when they arrive here. A jet Attacker was meant to be just stopping for lunch on Tuesday, en route for Karachi, but the pilot never realised that one wheel of his undercarriage had failed to come down, and as they never signalled anything wrong from the control tower, he brought a jet (mind you) plane in to land on one wheel!! Luckily for him the tank, which was ripped open, was carrying paraffin and not petrol, otherwise the whole thing would have burst into flames! He was quite unhurt and the plane damaged only fairly slightly, but of course quite incapable of going on. Jack has been putting him up and employing Isabel and myself to cheer him up – actually it has been the other way round. There was quite a flap on though, with cables flashing back and forward, as he has simply got to be in Karachi by Monday plus the Attacker for an air display. Also he was terrified they would give him the sack, as those jets are worth about 30 or 40 thousand pounds! However, all is well, and a mechanic arrived last night from Karachi, and another Test Pilot called Murray White arrives this afternoon on K.L.M., yet another – Brian Trubshaw – in a Valetta plus the spare parts tonight, and tomorrow another Attacker is being flown out by yet another Test Pilot…

Well, on Tuesday Isabel asked me to go to dinner with Jack, and I refused, but eventually she persuaded me and said the pilot was awfully nice, so in the end I accepted. I am so glad I did too, as he is terrific fun…I opened the door to Jack and the Pilot – and believe it or not – he is the spitting image of Michael Ibbetson on the Empress – the GORGEOUS

Captain!! His name is Davis Morgan – commonly known as Dave – and now known as 'One wheel Morgan'!!…I got on like a house on fire with Dave – unfortunately he is married! We had a most enlightening conversation after dinner about the Odyssey! Yesterday we three (Isabel, Pauline and myself) had all decided we must have an early night to prepare for tonight. So in the afternoon I didn't bother to have a rest, but washed and ironed for Cyprus! Then I went down to choir practice and got back about 8.00 p.m. to find that…Dave had invited himself along to have dinner with us! (So it was goodbye to hairwashing and early night!)…We had a very nice dinner, talking about ghosts! We sat talking until about midnight when Jack arrived from his dinner party to give Dave a lift home. Of course they both had drinks and we ended the evening playing liar dice and poker at about 2.00 a.m. I wish you could have seen Dave and me sitting on the carpet playing strip poker most intently! It was a fight to the death, but I won luckily!! (He only had to take two shoes off and then we decided to stop!). It was great fun though, and the first time I have played with my beautiful liar dice since the Empress!!'

Baghdad   *11 August 1950*

'I have actually sat in the cockpit of the jet 'Attacker' which won the S.B.A. (I don't know what that stands for!) Trophy the other day!! *What* an evening we had last night – phew!!…the phone rang to say the Valetta was stuck in Nicosia and would be coming on today. Five minutes later they rang again to say it was now on its way and would arrive at 11.50 p.m.!…Dave and Murray came back and Dave had some dinner. We all sat about and gossiped and then it was time to meet the Valetta – so we all decided to go and meet them!!…We got there in plenty of time, so Dave took us to the hangar to look at his jet. It is an amazing plane – fairly small – and the cockpit is simply *minute*!

I, with great difficulty, climbed up and inside and honestly you can only just fit in – it is just like sitting in a child's toy motor car. Your head is above the level of the plane – and when you move off you draw the glass top over you. But it must be terribly uncomfortable for long, as there is no room to even move your legs, and of course no-one else can even fit into the plane! Being a jet there is no time to use a parachute in an emergency, so the seat is so made that if anything happens and you want to get out in a hurry, you pull a little handle and you shoot up 80 ft. into the air, seat and all! Shot out with you are all sorts of useful things such as a rubber dinghy and sail, rations, parachute and even a fishing rod!! It is absolutely incredible! I was terrified I should pull the handle and suddenly disappear 80 ft. up through the hangar roof – but luckily it was detached or something. I jumped down via the wings with even more difficulty, but luckily Dave was there to pick up the bits! The whole plane is amazing, and it has sort of gills at the sides to take in the air – at the tail there is an enormous round hole out of which the air comes again. It looks to me just like an enormous vacuum cleaner – and I believe that is the general principle!

Saturday morning. Hullo – I'm still just alive after another glorious evening!…John Evans collected us three about 8.00 and we went to the British Club. It is a terribly nice club, and has a lovely English atmosphere inside. Normally ladies are not allowed into the bar, but only into the lounge. However last night was a special sort of guest night, and we were allowed into the holy of holies!! There is a large air-conditioned and terribly comfortable lounge into which ladies are allowed if they are honorary members, and there is also a very nice ladies' room and little dining room where you can get food to eat at any time up to 1.30 a.m. Jack Sallis is making Pauline, Isabel and myself honorary members which will be terribly nice. We don't pay any subscription or anything, but just put in a dinar or so to a credit account and sign chits until that is finished. It will really be terribly nice and useful, as it is in Rashid Street and one can go there when tired after shopping or something.

The other two pilots – Les Colquhoun and Brian Powell – arrived a bit later, and we all had a nice supper of chops, chips and peas…Dave, Isabel and myself were very keen to go to the Abdullah, so we eventually badgered Jack into taking us all along…Dave was absolutely tireless and in grand form – he wanted to go on to Ici Paris and stay up till five – but as he was flying the 'Attacker' today, we insisted that he should go to bed! We really had quite a time persuading him! I danced a lot with him and he really was a dear – he just *couldn't* have been nicer. I also danced with Brian Powell – he was rather after Michael's stature – and dark too. He danced extremely well, and was awfully nice too. We all sat and talked a lot and it was lovely. Dave was telling me what wonderful sights he sees – and (what rather surprised me) that the scenery etc. compensated for everything! So it can't be all that fun flying. He says you can see two sunrises – and once he went through a rainbow so that the arc made a complete circle round the plane! He was awfully interesting about it all – and from what I can gather this Test Pilot business takes a tremendous lot out of you – even for a short time in the air…

Today he was up at 5.30 a.m. and they went down to the Airport early to try out the plane. Apparently he went up about 7.30 a.m., but this time his undercarriage stuck *down* and he couldn't get it up! So he landed again, and it was a matter of a few hours before they put that right. We had arranged that he would do his test flight over Air Lodge so that we could dash up onto the roof and have a look. So he found it on the map and everything. Unfortunately when he did the test flight I was out visiting Thomas Cook's. I was just coming back in the car when I heard it – I just had time to fling myself out of the back window and see the silver plane twisting and turning all over the place – then in a flash it was gone! I got back and Isabel had had quite a good view. However I was rewarded as just now he set off for good, and flew over Air Lodge again (quite out of the way!). I tore up onto the roof and he went over really quite slowly and we could see his head and everything. Then he went up and up and away towards Basra and his next stop…

Now I've met quite a number of these test pilots it really does hit one how exceptionally nice they all are, and they seem of a very high calibre indeed. I suppose they must all have something extra to enable them to carry on. I wouldn't have missed the experience for anything. They seem quite different from the normal run of people in Baghdad…

Baghdad   *14 August 1950*

'…The Valetta came back yesterday on its way home, but only stayed about an hour. Jack went down to meet them and apparently it was jolly lucky they did follow after the Attacker as they had more trouble with it at Sharjah! However, to all our great reliefs, Dave plus Attacker have arrived safely in Karachi – and in time too! Today he is doing his big display – I do hope all goes well…

Then last night we went for our usual Sunday dinner party with Jack. Neville Dowding materialised at last – and for once my second impression was even better than the first!! He is a *very* nice man. Absolutely stunningly good-looking – and awfully well-kept – you know the sort of look!! He really was most amusing – and made the most killing faces. We had a lovely dinner – ending up with meringues! Then we just sat and talked until about midnight. He is most intelligent – and was rather depressing about the Korean question. We took him home in the car and deposited him safely at the Mess. Everyone else liked him too – you see I have excellent taste!!…

P.S. Jack says that Dave was really quite worried about me

going to Cyprus all by myself, and was afraid I'd be rather lonely. Oh! dear – he *was* nice – it will take a holiday in Cyprus for me to recover from his niceness!! He was tall – thin – terribly good-looking with a sort of 'interesting' face. Jack says he was awfully shaken after landing on one wheel – can you wonder?! Anyway he congratulated me on having cheered him up!!'

★　　★　　★

On Board the Empress of Australia.

View from our roof in Baghdad.

My roofbed.

Female Staff House.

Pat, Padre, Isabel and I.

Babylon; The Hittite Lion.

Bakr and Tamr, cook and boy.

Air Lodge, Baghdad.

CHAPTER 4

Cyprus, Kyrenia and Beirut
23.08.50 - 03.09.50

Mary was entitled to 14 days 'local leave' a year. There was no hill station nearby to get away from the heat of the Baghdad summer. So in 1950 Mary chose to spend a fortnight in the Mediterranean. She went by Nairn bus across the desert to Beirut, where as a result of introductions she was able to stay at the St George's Club. Then she flew to Cyprus, and stayed at Nicosia and Kyrenia, where she met up with Jane Mitchell, one of the Embassy girls from Baghdad. She did plenty of sightseeing and had a full social life as usual; also as usual her travels and social life are fully recorded in letters to her parents. She returned to Baghdad by the same route. In the extracts from her letters that follow, only comments that relate to her life in Iraq are recorded.

★   ★   ★

The Dome Hotel, Kyrenia, Cyprus   *23 August 1950*

'Guess who was in the bar yesterday evening before dinner?! Peter!!! I can't remember his surname, but he is a 1st Lt. in the Oxford and Bucks. Light Infantry and was on board the *Empress* coming out! Do you remember, he was the one who asked the nice lady to introduce him to me!! I knew he was stationed in Cyprus but I never thought I'd meet him. The strange thing was that he has sailed for England today in the Empress from Limassol – so I only just caught him. I walked into the bar and he turned round and recognised me at once, which was pretty good!! It was terribly funny as he tried to

65

introduce me to his friends, but all he could remember was 'Baghdad' – as apparently I was known throughout the *Empress* as 'Baghdad'!…'

The Dome Hotel, Kyrenia   *26 August 1950*

'Thank you so very much for your wonderful letters. I laughed and laughed over 'Archie smiler' 'Boot-black' etc. etc.!!! When I get back to 'Baggers' I will do my best to compile a complete and up-to-date 'directory' of my friends!!…'

The Dome Hotel, Kyrenia   *30 August 1950*

'Last night I bought Homer's Odyssey which I have been meaning to read for ages. Dave was reading it – and said I simply must read it. He would have left me his copy, but didn't finish in time!…'

St George's Club, Beirut   *3 September 1950*

'Eleven years since the war started – isn't it amazing? I can remember it so clearly too – coming out of church and being told. We just *can't* be in for another can we? What are people thinking of? We just *can't* have another war. Nobody does anything – just carries on with their drinking. I am sure if people pulled themselves together it could be averted. Last Sunday evening we went to the only service of the day – and of all the hundreds of British etc. staying in Kyrenia only Glubb Pasha and family were in church besides ourselves. I went this morning at 8.00 to the little church next door to the Club. The service was taken by a Lebanese – who sounded alright if you didn't look at him. There were five of us in church! Oh dear! – what a depressing letter! Sorry – but it comes over one all at once and makes one furious. It is just the same in Baghdad –

even with an excellent Padre. Of the 1,000 odd British and 150 Americans in Baghdad – there are only two or three at communion. The Ambassador never enters the church at all – nor do any of the Embassy staff, except for Philip Mallet – who is a 3rd Secretary – lowest of the low! What an example – and we are supposed to be a Christian country. Can anyone wonder why we have lost our prestige the world over? All foreigners see us doing is drinking – and that is all a good many people do. Gosh! I must stop – I'm getting angrier and angrier!…

Well. Back to work on Tuesday. Cyprus was divine – absolutely perfect – and ranks with Switzerland as the ideal spot for a honeymoon! Beirut is pleasant – but no fun alone. I would rather just stay here and be lazy than go exploring. No more leave till next year – but it will be quite nice to get back to 'Baggers'! I only wish I was coming home and could tell you all about my impressions of everything. One thing I have promised myself that I shall never, never, marry anyone but a Britisher…

…By the way you *did* realise that Dave is married with three children – didn't you? I wondered because you said you'd expect that I'd hear from him. Well, I shan't and anyway I wouldn't want to really. He was quite one of the nicest men I have ever met – but its just one of those things that can't be helped. He will just be a very pleasant memory for some time to come…'

★   ★   ★

CHAPTER 5

Baghdad
09.09.50 - 16.12.50

Baghdad   *9 September 1950*

'Well, here I am back at the old typewriter again…

On Tuesday evening…I was asked to a very small party – and
Pat and myself were the only females. Archie was there and we
talked for ages – but I have quite recovered now and gaze at
him with dispassionate eye – even that smile fails to arouse any
emotion!!…Derek Johnson was also there. I am sure you have
heard of him – but in case you haven't he is in the R.O.C.
[Rafidain Oil Company] aged 24 – ex-Navy – dark, and of the
same build as Michael [Clapp]! Actually he is *very* like Michael
– only a rather untidier loose-limbed edition. He is very nice
anyway and most amusing…After the party he asked Pat and
me home to supper. It was just marvellous!! It was really
homelike – there seemed to be nothing much to eat and we
had great fun frying eggs and bacon! If you could have seen
Derek ripping up bacon in his hands! I found I could hardly
remember how to fry an egg!!…

Derek Johnson asked me to a party given by an R.O.C. man
and his wife called O'Sell. It was…One of the pleasantest
evenings I've had. We got very hilarious and played all sorts of
silly games…It was all terribly amusing. Then they tied Derek
and me together with string and there was a special way of
getting undone! It was such a nice change from purely sitting
and drinking! About 1.40 a.m. we went on to the Havana…
When it closed we pushed on the 'Ici Paris' until that closed
about 4.15 a.m.!!! It was fun there – I danced a lot with Derek

and like him more and more. We got on very well together and I hope he still thinks I am 'good value'! Pat and I eventually got into bed about 4.45 a.m.!...'

Baghdad   *15 September 1950*

'I went to the Sworder's party on Tuesday night and enjoyed it for a short time – but then it was pure H - - L!!! We had drinks and a wonderful buffet supper – then dancing. Max Reynolds said he would give Ursula, myself and another girl a lift home whenever we wanted. But you know how it is – I was just panting to go – and one of the others would be dancing. I nearly went mad – and was on the point of getting a taxi and taking myself home. Philip Mallet was the only one who kept me sane. He is nice. He offered to run me home in the Flying Bomb – but I couldn't really as he hadn't even got it with him – and we were *miles* in the opposite direction. However he *was* nice – and at least had good manners. I can't understand these men who deliberately keep you up against your will!! How I envied Jane Mitchell with Kenneth to whisk her away when she spoke the word. That's the worst of being all on one's own – you just *can't* get away. It is the height of rudeness too, (out here!) to call yourself a taxi. Apparently Pauline did it last week at a party and slipped away without anyone knowing – and they were livid after!! Can't people *see* you look tired and want to go?!...'

Baghdad   *18 September 1950*

'I simply adored the dance at Habb. Archie and Sheila gave me a lift down (in Archie's new car)...I danced a lot with Butts and we saw all sorts of nice people – it really was fun. There was an excellent buffet supper about midnight and afterwards Jimmy insisted on champagne! Honestly, it is the *only* drink, isn't it? I really feel fine after it and can keep awake and even be moderately amusing! Best of all, it doesn't make you feel ill next morning! After a bit I wandered over and paid a visit to Pat and Peter Hughes – it was great fun as for some reason I was on top of my form and every time I opened my mouth they went off into peals of laughter!! Eventually I thought I had better go back to Butts. To my joy he was dancing and there was Archie all alone! We had a simply lovely dance – and I think he is GORGEOUS again!! He was rather surprised at me, I think. I don't think he thought I'd got it in me to be amusing. Anyway it was a wonderful evening. The dance was over about 3.00 and I immediately set to work with vigour to find someone to drive Ursula and myself home. (Archie and Co. were staying). Dicky Bird said he'd take us home when we wanted. Well, imagine the difficulty I had persuading all these people they must go as soon as possible! They all wanted to go to bed and leave at 5.00 a.m. Well, I knew that would have been quite fatal – as to start with, no-one would have woken up! Gosh, I badgered and bullied – (I didn't know I had it in me!) and eventually by 4.30 a.m., Dicky, another man, Ursula, Brian Fox-Male, Pat Comber and myself were on the road to Baghdad. It was some feat getting them all there – I can tell you…I don't think I have ever spent quite such an uncomfortable car journey. There were four of us in the back – and I started off on Brian's knee – however, I eventually slid down and sat on the floor with my head on his knee and believe it or not I went to sleep in that position for quite half an hour! It certainly was a mad journey – but we all got back safe and sound. (I was rather worried we'd all crash or something – after having badgered them all to come!). I walked into the house at 6.15 a.m. just as Pauline had got up! I had a bath and changed and had breakfast and was quite at my most wide-awake on the way to the office. I told Mr Ray, and he hadn't any idea I'd even gone! I felt fine for the first hour or so, but after then I had to consume quantities of strong coffee to stop my eyes glazing! My goodness, on Saturday night I was in bed by nine and slept until 8.40 a.m. the next morning (on the roof too!). This is the first time I have actually missed one whole night of sleep, and I don't think I shall do it often. The funny thing is I have felt so much better ever since!…'

Baghdad   *25 September 1950*

'Great joy!! At last our house has been put on the 'phone and our number is Baghdad *3268*. Do you know they applied last August – in 1949 – and we have only just got it?! Anyway it is a great joy – as it really was rather grim before. We couldn't even ring up for a taxi or ring up and get out of a party or anything!!

…I had to dash back and go to a party at Max Reynolds'. It was rather horrible (for me!) as usual, as it was mostly Americans. Pauline was there too, but she enjoyed herself…I talked to a very nice married man called Tony Stuart-Williams. However, he would keep calling me 'naïve' instead of Mary, which annoyed me intensely. He says a lot of people do in Baghdad – I wish they wouldn't because I'm not anyway. People *are* SILLY. I have come to the sad conclusion that I don't enjoy parties at all, and that it is only the PEOPLE that I enjoy talking to. The result is that if I go to a party and there is no-one there I particularly like, then I don't enjoy myself and vice-versa. Now, tonight should be a lot of fun, as there are heaps of people I like coming. But it is a worry, isn't it? The awful thing is that people keep on telling me (in a roundabout way) and Pauline etc. how terribly nice I am etc. etc., refreshing and what have you – but they can't *really* like me. What am I to do? The rather pleasant thing is that I don't worry so long as I still enjoy the Philip, Nigel, Neville people etc., and their parties. Also (I suppose it must be a sign of increasing years and wisdom!), I don't feel miserable when Pauline goes out and I don't. That is a thing I thought I could never get used to, but I must admit I feel very relieved now. It is a nice comfortable feeling when you give up worrying, and I don't think I get quite as jealous as I used to – at least I hope not!…'

Baghdad   27 September 1950

'RUN and get out your chart of 'Baggers eligibles' – and change Neville Dowding's to DE LUXE!!!! Everything is right again – and my inferiority complex etc. etc. have all disappeared like the wind. Ain't life fun?!!

Well, to start at the beginning. Pauline's party was a great success – at least I thought so. She is a bit worried it wasn't, as she thought it was a bit quiet and proper, but after all a cocktail party is a cocktail party – even in Iraq! The roof really did look delightful in the moonlight. We had all our beds out there and a few chairs etc. for people to sit on – also rugs little tables and lamps. It looked very nice – the eats were excellent, and there was plenty of drink! She had had a little wooden bar made, which we can use anywhere as it is quite light – and really lends tone to a party!…

Then suddenly a voice said, 'hello' – and there was Neville just arrived, looking as though he had been doing anything but flying from 7.00 a.m. to 7.00 p.m.! I got him a drink – and said that I must start introducing him to people – but he said, 'No' – and believe it or not, from the moment he walked in until the end, he just stayed with Derek and me…After a bit, the last of the people left (that is except for Neville, Derek and Jimmy Butts – the latter who was up in Baghdad for the night). So we five (Pauline, myself and the aforementioned) clambered back on the roof – and rested our aching limbs. Then they suggested we should go to the 'Abdullah' and see the cabaret! It was too good to believe – and I had to keep pinching myself in case I was dreaming…Neville asked me for a dance right away…After the cabaret I danced more with Neville, and then Derek, then Neville, then Derek, and so on the entire evening, with an occasional one with Jimmy. It was absolute heaven – a perfect evening – and quite restored my faith in mankind – myself – and everyone else. A Good Thing once in a way – don't you agree? Anyway, Neville is quite definitely THE one at the moment – and in fact the one and only in Baghdad. Even Archie had faded far away!…Going home in the car was even more fun than coming!! I had Derek's head on one shoulder and Neville's on the other. (Luckily I had washed my hair in Evan William's and it smelt rather nice!). Anyway, it was a pleasant drive – and far too short!…I trod on air all yesterday and am just descending today! The tragedy is that one never sees Neville, but in a way that is a good thing, because you *do* get so sick of seeing the same people at party after party. I think he *likes* me, which is something – but it is difficult to tell. Also, apparently almost every girl falls for him – but he *very* rarely takes anyone out or anything like that. However, it was so lovely on Monday that that will last me for some time!…'

Baghdad   *5 October 1950*

'Guess who arrived on Monday?! Dave Morgan!! It was rather funny actually as I was sound asleep on Monday afternoon, when I was suddenly woken to hear Isabel yelling in my ear that Dave Morgan was coming to tea! We had heard a jet over in the morning – and jokingly said that that must be Dave. But actually we thought he'd gone home from Karachi ages ago. He has been out there for about two months demonstrating with the Attacker, while they have been making up their minds about the next one. He is now on his way home taking this Attacker back, and then he has to fly the next one out again in about a fortnight. He had tried to ring us up at Air Lodge, but we had already left the office. Of course he thought that we still weren't on the phone, and so he had a terrific game trying to ring up various numbers to find out where we lived. After trying the British Institute, and various other places, he found 'Embassy Staff House – female' in the book and thought that sounded familiar. Luckily he got Sheila Davis who put him onto our number…We packed him off in the end as he was flying to Cairo next day. So, with many farewells, off he went. However next morning there was a noticeable silence in the air – and about lunch-time the phone went – Dave – of course he was staying until Wednesday morning as something had gone wrong again!!…On Tuesday evening he was in a 'party' mood, and so we got Derek Johnson along to make a fourth. Of course Dave and Derek got on like a house on fire – they had both been in the Fleet Air Arm – and found that everyone they mentioned was a mutual acquaintance. They were just like a couple of schoolboys – with their reminiscences! Anyway it was a highly successful combination!! At about 11.10 p.m., just as we were thinking that Dave ought to be going home to bed, they insisted we should go to the Abdullah. So we packed off there and saw the cabaret – it is a new one and really very good. We had a most hilarious evening – Dave was in grand form – and we just had to remove the gin from his reach in the end!…We got home eventually and felt none too good yesterday morning! Dave told us he would be airborne at 7.30 a.m. Well, we reached the office about 7.45 a.m. and thought he couldn't possibly have gone yet. We heard nothing all morning and began to get rather worried, wondering what effect the gin might have had! However, all was well as we rang up and found he had got off already at 7.30 a.m. sharp. Do you know he is only about 25 or 26 – although he looks much more. He was married when he was about 20 or so. It is such fun meeting all these interesting people. I do enjoy it so…'

Baghdad   *7 October 1950*

'…Great excitement! Pauline and I are going up to Mosul for next weekend. We rang up John Burgess of the Information Service up there (who I met once at a party!). He remembered me – and cottoned on at once, saying could he look after us…'

Baghdad   *9 October 1950*

'Just had a most lovely weekend! Ain't life fun??!! Well, to start at the beginning – Oh! no! – I must tell you about the weather. It has actually been *COLD*!! Last night it really was cold sitting out on the lawn at the Club. I had a cardigan on and even then it was cold. Last night on the roof I very wisely took out my second blanket and was beautifully warm. But when I woke up this morning it was simply lovely as I was warm as toast inside, but my nose was all cold and outside the bedclothes it was FREEZING!…

Yesterday, which I was really rather dreading, was simply marvellous! The Isas (that is an Iraqi family who are Christian and great friends of the Padre's) collected me at 7.30 a.m…We picked up Pat Godfrey and then set off for Habbaniya…After church we all (Isas, Pat and I) went down to the lake for the rest of the day. I have never been there before in all the time I have been out here, and I certainly have missed a lot!! It is about five miles from Habb. And suddenly you come between two hills and see it spread out before you. It is simply ENORMOUS, and just like coming upon the Mediterranean or something. You can't see across it and it is about 15 miles wide and 40 miles long – so you see it really is a large lake. It is fresh water, but is so blue it looks just like the sea. I was simply overjoyed by it and can't think *why* people don't go there more often. It was just like spending a day at the sea and I feel so WELL today! There is a tiny little boat club there where all the sailing dinghies etc. are moored, but we couldn't go in not being members. However, we went about a mile along the shore and parked the car. It is quite sandy all round the edge, though there is a lot of mica in the rocky parts. We changed (with great difficulty!) and had a swim before lunch, then we were so *hungry* we just had to sit down to our lunch at 12.00!! Pat and I had brought our own, but the Isas were most indignant and said we shouldn't have done any such thing. My goodness! They produced their 'picnic' and I have never seen so much food in all my life. Talk about a picnic – it would have done admirably as a buffet supper for a dance consisting of about 20 couples!! They had plates of chicken, eggs, potatoes, beans, stuffed onions and tomatoes, various little bits and pieces, meat pies and goodness knows what! We ate and ate, and then I produced my bananas and grapes, thinking they hadn't brought any! But my goodness – they had bananas three times as large, and great bunches of grapes that made mine look puny!! The only thing they were grateful for was my coffee, carefully brought in Uncle John's thermi!! After lunch we could hardly move, but we sat just in the water while Mr Jamil Isa told our fortunes. He is actually *very* good indeed, and has a terrific reputation out here. A lot of the things he said about character were very true, but he said some killing things otherwise. I am going to marry someone of an upper class – so either I'm destined for the Hon. David Herbert, or else he thinks I'm a barmaid anyway! I am going to marry when I am about 22 or 23, and have a boy and then a girl. But he didn't say anything else about the husband – nothing like the 'tall, dark, stranger' stunt! It was simply lovely by the lake, because although the sun was hot there was a very cool wind, which just saved us! I got very sun-burnt but luckily not painfully or anything like that! Pat and I became filled with energy and rushed up and down the shore – working off our enormous lunch! We finally left about 2.45 p.m…'

Baghdad   *18 October 1950*

'We start winter hours on Monday – which entails working from 8.00 a.m. – 2.00 p.m.! We aren't going to do our two days a week 8.00 a.m. – 4.30 p.m. – unless there is a lot of work. They had to all last winter, but there is so little work now it doesn't look as though we shall have to very often – which is fine. We do the same number of hours as the summer – but the Embassy, who do *less* hours, have the most dreadful plan: they work from 9.00 – 1.00 and then come back again from 4.30 – 6.30 p.m. – which I think is horrid…

By the way, Neville Dowding is the nephew of *the* Dowding – known as 'Stuffy' Dowding. He is an Air Chief Marshal and did tremendous things in the war and really is quite famous! I haven't seen Neville again – which is sad – but I have been getting on so well with Derek it doesn't matter…

P.S. In ever such a good mood this morning after last night. Derek is so nice!!…'

Baghdad   *17 October 1950*

'…Now, I really must start on Mosul. We had a simply *perfect* weekend and it just couldn't have been nicer. John Burgess was kindness itself and couldn't possibly have given us a better time…

We were in a 4-berth cabin and thought we were getting it to ourselves, when a large Iraqi lady came in at the last moment. However she was very pleasant. The trains are excellent – and the 2nd Class really *was* comfortable and clean. It might have been a 1st Class carriage. We undressed and washed, ate our sandwiches, drank our coffee and proceeded to settle down for an early night. Over the window (inside) was a sort of netting with tin outside, which is meant to keep the dust out. However we didn't trust it and decided to close the window as well. So

Pauline wound away – but of course we discovered in the morning that instead of shutting it she had opened it wide! We had not a bad night considering – but in the morning of course we were just covered in dust!! It was *terrible* – and I haven't got it out of my lungs yet!!…

We arrived in Mosul early – about 7.00 a.m. – and John Burgess was on the station to meet us very kindly. He left us at the Station Hotel, where we had an excellent breakfast…About 9.00 a.m. we went to his house and there met a very interesting lady called Barbara Parker. She is secretary to Professor Mallowan – the archaeologist (married to Agatha Christie!!) who is excavating Nimrud in the spring…She took us round Mosul in the car and we saw the suq. Mosul is on the Tigris – and very similar to Baghdad – though it is smaller and *far* less civilised. The smells are appalling! But it is a pleasant little town. The suq was fun – but nothing 'local' or interesting to buy really – just the usual Lifebuoy soap etc!!

On Sunday…We went to Aqra!! Wasn't it lucky, especially after hearing all about it from Derek!! We went past Nineveh again – but luckily we stopped and went to see the Winged Bulls – which is really all there is to see now. They were magnificent and how well I remember them in my history book. It was nice having Barbara as she could answer all my questions about Sennacherib etc. etc! Nimrud was apparently the capital of Assyria before Nineveh. I must read it all up anyway, as it was most interesting. We also saw what is meant to be Jonah's tomb – but definitely isn't!! After that we set out for Aqra – and it was quite different. The country was much wilder, bleak and rugged. You really felt brigands would come dashing round the next corner. In fact all the Kurds etc. up there are armed to the teeth with the most villainous-looking weapons!! It took about $2^{1}/_{2}$ hours to get to Aqra – and it is the most amazing village. It is built right at the foot of these rugged mountains and all the houses are built in terraces all the way up. When we first arrived we were all ushered in to be introduced to the Qaimaqam. He is the sort of Lord Mayor of the village – so we all trooped up and sat in a row facing him, sipping diminutive cups of Turkish coffee. Then John tried to get us away – but the Qaimaqam had already ordered tea. This we sipped out of 'one-size larger' cups and it really was delicious! After meeting him (he was a nice dignified man) we were taken round the suq by a couple of Kurds. I bought two painted cane cigarette-holders about two feet long (!) and also a little embroidered cotton Kurdish cap!! For lunch we went to the waterfall a little way away, which is a real beauty spot. It is a very high thin waterfall if you know what I mean – and was really beautiful. We had lunch there and paddled and afterwards walked all round the top of it and down through the back of the village. It really was most interesting, and I believe typical of mountain villages in Tibet, Kashmir and elsewhere. On the way back the men did some more shooting – mostly Chikors (sort of partridge) and black partridge. We treated John and Tony to dinner at the Hotel (very expensive!!) as we really felt we must repay them somehow…We…Caught the train at 9.00 p.m. This time we paid the odd 300 fils each and had an air-conditioned carriage and it certainly was worth it!!…'

Baghdad   *20 October 1950*

'…After choir practice, Bill gave Derek, Carol Cooke and I a lift back to the club, and we went in for a 'quick' drink! Of course it was quite fatal and I didn't get home until 3.00 a.m.! (Derek thought we should make it a weekly institution after choir practice, but I think otherwise!!). Anyway, we sat in the bar (only because it is too cold outside and anyway there was hardly anyone else there – not really a wicked place you know!). Then we had bar suppers and were joined by Johnny Forder and Dick Stubbs. It developed into quite a party…Everyone got very cheerful as the evening progressed, so when the bar closed we went off to Dick's house and played poker dice for a bit. Carol had never played, and they just couldn't believe that I had played before. So when I came out talking about 'full house – aces on jacks' etc. they were flabbergasted! I got terribly sleepy so I went to sleep on the sofa and the others gradually gave up the game and sprawled around the room. Derek sat on the floor with his head on my shoulder! Johnny however was still full of life and hopping round the room. (Needless to say he wasn't flying the next day!). I eventually managed to persuade them to take me home and was carried bodily out to the car by Derek!! To my surprise I felt fine in the office yesterday morning…'

Baghdad   *29 October 1950*

'…I have got to continue being Mess Secretary for *three* months! Isn't it dreadful, but no doubt very good for me. We started having 'servant' problems as Pauline rather gets their backs up as she is always nagging, and so we have decided that just one person should be in charge of the house and voice all the complaints. We do it for three months at a time as then the cook etc., know where they are. He [the cook] is much happier now and most willing. I hope all will be well – but I *would* have to do it now with Christmas, party etc. and everything at once! Still, it isn't all that bad, and think what good practice it is!…

You haven't mentioned Derek *once* in your letters. I am so disappointed. Don't you think he sounds terribly nice?!!!! I do like your comments on my friends. By the way, could you move him up one place to 'de luxe' in the chart?!!!…

Baghdad   *30 October 1950*

'…Saturday night – Pauline's river party – which was a

roaring success and great fun. I will tell you all about it first, and then end up with Derek's and my talk! Well, Derek came and collected Isabel and myself and also John Mawer and a girl-friend of his, and took us all down to the assembly spot on the river bank. We all looked wonderful!! I had on a red blouse and my old grey skirt, and that blue cardigan of Auntie Elsie's that does right up to the neck, red sandals, and took with me a couple of old R.A.F. blankets for extra warmth. Isabel was similarly attired with a wonderful old R.A.F. mac on top of it all – just too alluring we looked! Most of the women wore slacks, and the men all wore old suits etc. Derek looked just MARVELLOUS!! He had on baggy old corduroy trousers, with his pyjama legs on underneath tucked into his socks for extra warmth, and on top he had a shirt, sweater and coat with a wonderful scarf round his neck and a pipe! The pipe just made it and he looked divine – rather scruffy – but only tousled sort of scruffy – not dirty scruffy!! (Like Daddy going to the bath in the early morning – adorable!). Anyway we got to the right spot and of course had to hang around for hours, while people arrived and finished off with cocktail parties etc. We spent the time packing all the food, drink and blankets etc. into the launch. It was an old motor launch of a reasonable size. There was a covered bit in the bows where we stored all the drinks etc. and set up the bar (!), and then going towards the stern there was the engine, and then a little place with two wooden seats, and then the stern part. It was all covered in, and you could go on the roof. It was flat and stretched the whole length of the boat, so it was ideal for sitting on. We spread blankets and everyone pretty well sat up there. We finally got everything stowed away, Isabel's torch being the only casualty as Derek dropped it into the river! We finally got underway about 8.30 p.m. and set off down stream. Derek was simply wonderful and worth his weight in gold. He organised everything and helped Pauline do the drinks – and was just marvellous. (The Navy every time – Michael is quite right about landlubbers' inability to co-operate!). Most of the other men were quite helpless, and lolled about the deck. They had even brought a gramophone, which shocked me to the marrow, but then it was a half American party – and you have to allow for these things! They started dancing on the top – and we stayed down below dishing out drinks etc. It was a wonderful journey down and the river looked simply wonderful! It took about an hour to get there, and being a cold night it was terribly funny as several people wanted to spend pennies! Once again the Navy saved the situation. Derek found an old tin which he put in the stern part for the 'ladies', and then managed to tactfully get rid of people – and guard the way…When we got near the island, of course, everyone lolled over onto one side of the boat, and there were Derek, myself, and one or two other sober types – hanging on for grim death on the opposite side. We landed safely anyway, and people even managed to negotiate the narrow gang-plank! It was a bare sandy island, and we all settled down to getting the stores out again. The servants lit a fire and started cooking the Masquf, while Derek, Pauline and I washed glasses, and did the drinks! It was terrific fun – and we had a marvellous evening. Of course it was about 10.00 p.m. before the fish was ready, and we all lay around in an enormous circle wrapped in blankets…The fish arrived at last, and we all fell to. Oh! It was good as we were so hungry. By the end of supper, looking around you have never seen such a debauched looking scene in your life!! There were various somnolent bodies strewn about, and most people were a bit sleepy. I felt simply fine and wide awake – and so did Derek. I drank quite a bit of whisky to keep out the cold, and it did the trick as I was wonderfully warm…We finally packed up about 3.00 and got everyone on somehow – I still can't believe we didn't leave someone behind, but apparently not!

The journey home was wizard – having got everyone safely on we found (Derek and I) a nice spot to sit at the very end of the roof over the stern of the boat. Most other people flopped about and went to sleep, but Derek and I sat wrapped in blankets, and talked and talked solidly for an hour and a half all the way home!! We had a terribly interesting conversation, and he was terribly nice. I do like Derek as he is so natural, healthy and nice – and no funny business about him. He said a lot of terribly nice things about me in an ordinary way – I mean he really meant them, and wasn't being silly or anything. He said I was terribly lucky as I had looks (?!) as well as 'bags of personality'. Wasn't that last remark nice? I always thought that maybe I didn't have any personality at all. He says I have a good deal more common sense than the average girl of my age, and that it is doing me a lot of good being abroad…In fact he said SO MANY NICE THINGS that my head is really quite swollen, and it has boosted my 'ego' no end!! He said that he betted when I got home I should have heaps of proposals in my first three months – but I know better. He gave a wonderful description of the man I shall marry – he is apparently going to be 6 ft. 3 ins at least, play rugger every Saturday, and a jolly good party every Saturday night…We talked of heaps of other things – about the problem of Isabel for one. He says there is nothing one can do about her saying she will never marry. He says he knew a girl at home who was the friend of a girlfriend of his, and she was just the same. So he thought he really would make an effort and take her out, and give her a jolly good time. So he did, and apparently it was absolutely misery and neither of them enjoyed it in the least! He also talked about getting married – and says it is the only thing…He also gave me the gist of (his idea) the sort of girl men want to marry – and it seems that after all our worrying, I may stand a chance!! A sense of humour is the great thing, I believe, and he said I had that (Bother, I have got to do a letter)…

(Also, I'll tell you something else in strict confidence – shall I – yes! That night when Isabel and I went to Dick's and Derek's, I was looking at pictures of Cambridge in Derek's dressing room, and he kissed me – but most important of all I *liked* it for the first time in my life!).

By the time we reached Baghdad we both knew a good deal more about each other, which is a good thing. I didn't get to bed till 4.30 a.m. and do you know Isabel and I managed to get up and go to the early service?!…

P.S. You won't suddenly jump to the conclusion I'm *in love* with Derek or anything, will you? I assure you it is just an ordinary friendship – but so nice!'

Baghdad   *3 November 1950*

'We started our Arabic lessons last night, and I was most favourably impressed by the teacher and his way of conducting the lesson. Isabel and I went, and I suppose there must have been about five or six other women and one man – none of whom we knew. Anyway we registered ourselves as 'Students of the Iraq Institute' and all settled down at little desks. (My – it took me back!). The teacher is a very nice man, and obviously very clear in his mind as to what he is teaching us, and as to how far he is to go in each lesson. He came in and first taught us the 'Salaam', and then he had a basket of cups, saucers, forks etc. and proceeded to teach us their names. He went pretty quickly through, and we just wrote down the names in rough, phonetically in English so that we could pronounce them. He was good though, and by the end we were saying 'that fork in basket' and so on. (There is no verb 'to be' in Arabic). Then for the second half of the lesson we started to learn the script. I didn't realise we were going to learn that as well, and I am jolly glad now. It is simply fascinating and easier than it looks, and as far as I can make out almost the same principle as shorthand!! I got on alright, as it is purely a case of remembering at the moment, which is one of my less weak points! But one couple were quite clueless – it was terribly funny! I am terribly glad I decided to learn now, as it is just MARVELLOUS to be really learning something again, and having to use one's brain a little…'

Baghdad   *8 November 1950*

'…On the way down [to choir practice] D[erek] said, 'Would I come into the Club for a little while after?' I agreed – but blow me – when choir practice was over I found that *only* Carol, Ursula and Pat Godfrey were also filled with the intention of coming to the Club as well!! It's not that I mind in the slightest – I'm very fond of them – but how they can all march in and have Derek buy them drink after drink and bar suppers just beats me! It's my one 'bee in my bonnet' about all that lot. I quite see that if someone *asks* you to come for a drink that's OK as it's their lookout. But just to walk in in cold blood, night after night, into the bar – I don't know how they've the face to!! Now *do* tell me if you think I'm right over this – because it worries me again and again! I am sure Derek loves us all round him – what man wouldn't – but that isn't the point. The point is that he spends a *tremendous* amount each evening – and I just don't think it's fair. He has just moved into his house – and is desperately trying to make it liveable in (which it certainly isn't at the moment!) by buying chair covers, rugs, carpets and in fact everything except the bare essentials which the R.O.C. supplies…

Ann James was out here with the Stubbs after leaving school. She is about 19 now – and is at Mrs Hosker's Secretarial College next door to St James'!! She was *terribly* nice – although I only knew her for a month – but she was exceptionally nice and Derek has got her photo in his room and writes to her etc.

In fact I think he will marry her. It would be most suitable, actually...'

Baghdad   *16 November 1950*

...'About Derek: everything is ALRIGHT. It *is* just a friendship and nothing else. Funnily enough he said to me last night, 'You won't fall for me, will you?' And so we talked it all over – and he *is* so nice. He said although I am learning a tremendous lot out here, I won't meet very many men really – and it is *far* better to wait until one gets home again. But it is wonderful to be friends with him, as it is teaching me a tremendous lot of really interesting things. He has very kindly lent me a book on those sort of things, for which I am terribly grateful. It is a real good one, and has solved a lot of my 'worries', and removed all my 'fears' – which I think is excellent don't you? I always used to think certain things were 'nasty', but now I know it is wonderful if done at the proper time and place and not abused. In fact my whole outlook on marriage and married life etc. has changed and I feel confident I could make a success of it. I used to be terrified and appalled at the thought. I hope you don't mind me telling you all this – but you are the only person I can tell or would want to tell!!!...'

Baghdad   *18 November 1950*

'...I had some Araq for the first time in my life. It is the most amazing drink, as it looks just like water. You put a little in a glass and then add water, and it promptly goes all cloudy like Dettol!! It tastes and smells completely innocuous – rather like aniseed. However it is the sort of local wine and is most intoxicating if taken in large quantities. (I only had one glass!)'.

Baghdad   *25 November 1950*

'Ooooooh! What a week this has been!! I was in bed on
Sunday night by 10.15 p.m. but since then I have been out just
every single night, and also I haven't finished yet – tomorrow,
tonight, Monday and Tuesday are going to be nearly as bad!!...

Starting on Monday, I went to this tea party given by the Isas
to meet the Bishop...(Do you remember the Isas are the nice
Iraqis who Pat and I went down to Habb. with once, and had
that terrific picnic lunch!). Well, the tea was terrific, and with
my plate loaded with an enormous piece of plum cake I
thought I was safe, but to my horror that didn't appear to
matter and a great hunk of some cream cake was then plonked
on my plate! All the Miss Isas (four) had cooked different bits
of the tea etc. and we had to taste everything. The poor Padre
and Bishop had just been to a large lunch party at the Embassy,
and it was funny seeing them go slowly blue in the face over
the plum cake!! However, it was rather fun as Isabel and I
caused great amusement by spouting what Arabic we know!...
We eventually got away, and went to choir practice...Then, as I
told you, I was going out to dinner with the Taylor-Gills, a
very nice couple...We had a simply wonderful dinner and
eventually went off to the Abdullah to see the cabaret...we
ended up at Ici Paris, about 3.00 a.m., and had a most hilarious
time.

On Tuesday, Isabel and I went to Arabic, and then to
Ursula's, leaving the party at about 7.30...Ken asked me to
come back to eat partridge with them...

Wednesday was our last and final choir practice before the
Festival...We went back to the Club, had a bar supper, and then
were ready for the Scottish Reels practice at about 9.30 p.m.

On Thursday I really thought I had got an early night but it
was the opening night of the Select...It is far and away the best
night-club in Baghdad and the atmosphere is quite different.

You go in and you might almost be walking into a London hotel, as there are carpets on the floor and everything.

Then, last night, we had the Festival of Church Music… Afterwards we had this lovely party at Pat's house…

This morning we have just been entertaining – guess who?! The Royal Navy!! Three stokers from HMS WREN had to bring up a prisoner from Basra, and just called in at Air Lodge. What a thrill when we saw three pairs of real Bell-Bottoms walking about. We asked Philip if we could give them a beer, and so we did. Great delight as we were shown all the photos of girl-friends and what have you, and one came from West Hartlepool!!…

Tonight we are going to a dance at the British Club…

Then tomorrow I was asked to Habb. for the races, but just *must* have some time at home to do my Xmas presents, so I have refused that!…

Baghdad   *30 November 1950*

'…The other terrific thing that occurred over the weekend was that Mr de Courcy has suddenly become terribly fond of Pauline. It all boiled up on Saturday, as Isabel usually goes out shooting with him. However, he didn't go and never told Isabel anything about it. There was an awful strained atmosphere for a bit, before it really dawned on Isabel and me that he wasn't being rude to her, but had suddenly really fallen for Pauline. I must say I could hardly believe it, as I have always regarded him as a nice 'fatherly' man who we could call on in trouble – now, of course, he is the cause of all the trouble! Sunday was a strain, and Isabel looked *awful*! I got terribly worried about her. We both went to the early service at 8.00 and of course I had to tell her about Bill Hendrey [who had just died of a stroke], which just added to things. When we got back from church she was just about at breaking point, and mercifully spent the day with the Richmonds and the twins, and recovered. Of course, both Pauline and I thought she was miserable because Mr de Courcy was suddenly ignoring her. But actually she had seen exactly what was going to happen and was terribly worried. Mr de Courcy has asked Pauline to marry him. (Don't say anything to anyone, will you, as it is a terrible problem!). He is 55, and she is 29, but although we know that doesn't matter, it is a big decision to make. Apart from all that he is a widower, has a grown-up son of 24 who he doesn't get on with, and above all none of us (including Pauline) know anything about him at all. She admits that he never talks about himself, which I think is a great pity. Anyway, to my mind she isn't in love with him, and I am just terrified she might marry him out of pity. Actually, I know she is very fond of him, but keeps thinking of all the things she would miss by marrying him and all that sort of thing. Anyway, he has now gone away for ten days and she is left trying to decide what to do. Poor Pauline, what a problem...'

Baghdad   *4 December 1950*

'...I am getting on fine with Arabic, and am thoroughly enjoying it. It is just my cup of tea – practically all a case of memory! I was just asking Hanna, one of our interpreters, how to pronounce a certain word, and he suddenly looked at the rest of my Arabic! He said it was better than the teacher's copy – and called Ramzi over to look, who said it was 'amazing'. So obviously you have an infant prodigy daughter of Arabic!!...

On Friday I had an excellent game of squash with Pat Godfrey. We were terribly equal, but I just managed to beat her 5-4. It had been pouring with rain, and as I walked out of the squash court in my white shorts I suddenly sat plop down in about three inches of mud! It was the funniest sight imaginable! My racket and handbag were literally buried in mud, and my seat was a wonderful sight! I then had to stagger through the bar to get to the changing room, and of course ran into Hamish, Johnny and Co! Hamish, who is the keeper of my racket, was a pet and whisked it away as it was, and when I used it yesterday it had all been beautifully cleaned up!…

It certainly is a gay life, but I am still struggling along with my head above water, and things are still in their proper perspective – although you might not think so! (Parties are not the only thing in life!). Pauline and I had a great talk over breakfast the other day, and even she says I have blossomed out tremendously since she came – and grown up in my mind. Isn't life all a wonderful experience?

We are still in a turmoil about Pauline's Great Decision, and I don't know what she will decide…'

Baghdad   *7 December 1950*

'I am feeling so happy and cheerful this morning that I felt I must write and tell you! Actually by rights I suppose I should be in the depths of misery as Derek told me all about Ann James last night. However, I really *knew* all the time and it is a great relief now that we both know the other knows.

Well, anyway, we had been to a supper party with one of the R.O.C. people, and Derek brought me home after and came in and we talked for hours. I knew he had something on his mind, and so now everything is alright. He told me that he had been in love about four times before coming to Baghdad, but that it had all fizzled out. However, when he came out here and met Ann he just knew she was the one and only person, and as he said the 'bell clanged louder than ever before'. She, as you know, has gone home and is at Mrs Hosker's, and Derek really is in love with her and wants to get married in 1952 when he goes home. But he is terribly sensible and realises that anything might happen in the meantime. However at the moment it is alright, and I think it would be a *perfect* match for both of them. Anyway, all this came up because he was so frightened of hurting me. He was simply sweet and said that he was *terribly* fond of me, but that he didn't love me and knew I didn't love him. He said some terribly nice things about me too, so I don't feel in the least worried or anything! He asked if I minded just going on as we are – being great friends – but knowing that that is all. So it is marvellous – and just exactly as I want it too. What could be nicer – and none of those awful fears attached as to whether or not I'm in love with him, and whether or not he will propose etc. etc. So there will be none of those worries, but just someone nice to do things with while I'm here…'

Baghdad   *9 December 1950*

'…Oh! the B.O.A.C. Mess party was terrific fun and I did enjoy it. Oh! and I've fallen for Ralph Watts!! I just knew I would as he is very tall and FAIR!!! It is rather funny as of all people he was the first man I saw who was even young, let alone good-looking. I remember it was my first Saturday and Isabel had made up that party for the St George's Dance. I remember seeing Ralph then – and thinking that there must be *some* young men in Baghdad after all!! Anyway, of course one *never* sees him – even less of him than Neville – and except for a dinner party at Ken's once – and then our party – after both of which he was flying and had to go early, I had never really talked to him at all!…After supper they cleared away the tables and started dancing in the dining room…Ralph came along and whisked me off to dance saying, 'Just one Sir!' We danced for quite a long time actually and he is terribly nice…Anyway, I left with Derek about 1.45 a.m…

Yesterday afternoon I played tennis with Pat and who should also be playing tennis but Johnny and Ralph!! We had tea with them after – and then they went off to play snooker and Ralph said, 'Come along and watch' – so we did. I *do* like him! Oh! dear! Off I go again – could you put him up to de luxe please?!!! (How many is that now – we shall have to cross off some – Dave could go down actually!!)…

Baghdad   *16 December 1950*

'…Our great excitement of the moment is that Pauline is going to marry Michael de Courcy on December 31st!!! It has all been terribly sudden and she only eventually said 'yes' last Wednesday night! So I heard on Thursday and I still can't get used to the idea. Of course there is nothing that we can do now, and the only thing is to be very happy about it and make her feel it is all marvellous too. At any rate she is very happy about it herself and keeps on saying it is so marvellous to know she has done the right thing, so perhaps all will be well. It came as a terrible shock to most people, the majority of whom either don't know Michael or else never even knew she went out with him! Most people are rather naturally against it, but on the whole I hope it will work out alright. Philip Ray is very much against it and says she has been rushed etc., and that if she was under 21 he would not have allowed it, but of course he can do nothing now. The wedding is all fixed for the 31st and they are going off for a month, and then she hopes to continue working on her return, but I am very much afraid Head Office might not let her. Anyway back to two again in our house, which is very sad. The wedding is to be a very small private affair, and only Isabel, myself, the Stuart-Williams, and Michael's nephew and niece are to be present. She will be married in an ordinary suit and, of course, no bridesmaids or anything!…

Anyway it is all teaching me a tremendous lot and I only hope I won't suddenly do something crazy all in a hurry. If by any remote and possible chance I were to get engaged out here, either I would wait until the end of my contract and then go home to be married properly with you, or else break my contract like Pam Ballentyne, and go home. But I just couldn't get married all in a hurry like this, with no trousseau and none of the fun of being with one's parents etc. Anyway, I think one wants to get back to England anyway first, to get normal again, as it is definitely a life on its own out here. Still, I suppose it is all very well for me to talk now, but I do hope I shan't change my opinions or anything. At any rate it is not even remotely possible at present, so not to worry…'

★   ★   ★

CHAPTER 6

Baghdad
01.01.51 - 20.03.51

Baghdad   *New Year's Day 1951*

'…Jack took us down to Matins on Christmas morning and
the church really was full and it was a lovely service. Even H.E.
was there! After church we went over to the Iraqi Airways
Mess, had a drink and wished Neville and Johnny a Happy
Christmas! Ralph was flying…We stayed there about half an
hour and then went on to the British Club for about an
hour…We left actually before it really got 'rowdy', and arrived
at Derek's feeling very well indeed – on three sherries!!!…We
sat down to our Christmas lunch about 2.30 p.m…I went for a
blow and felt *much* better after that…I stayed until after the
King's speech. We didn't hear it *very* clearly, but he was very
good, wasn't he?…After that we started our 'rounds', and
dropping Isabel at Jack's en route, we went first to call on John
Mawer and Robin Witney…We left about 7.45 p.m. and our
next port of call was the Eddowes – a nice R.O.C.
couple!!…Next we popped into the Gaffneys next door and
were plied with drinks and food…About 10.30 p.m. or so we
went off to the Newlands, and eventually ended up at Kenneth
Hornby's about 11.30 p.m. What an evening. I have never done
that before – started drinking at 11.30 a.m. and continuing for
12 hours!! Actually I packed squashes in wherever possible and,
of course, the saving grace was that I was too full of food to
even manage a glass of water!!…People are so friendly and nice,
it was lovely…'

Baghdad   *6 January 1951*

'...My dear – history is in the making – Ralph has asked me out to dinner on Monday, followed by 'Hamlet' at the Railway Club!!! I didn't realise, but apparently it is the first time he has taken out *anyone* here!! Anyway I am in an awful panic now that I shall be dull, dumb, or just boring and *never* go again! However I shall be 'my natural self' and hope for the best!

...isn't it exciting?!!! I had to tell Derek all about it, and he was so nice and told me lots about Ralph as I don't really know him at all – never having spoken to him alone. He went to Epsom College, and left in 1938, so jut might have been there when we were there, and also might know Canon Powell! He is about 29, I think, and went straight into the Fleet Air Arm after leaving school, and is now B.O.A.C., of course.

Ain't life the most TREMENDOUS FUN?!! I am 'UP' at the moment, so be prepared next time for a tear-stained, miserable letter!! By the way, he is at least 6ft. 3ins. – *blonde*!! (at least fair!), terribly clever – good looking – and in fact just everything – wonderful swimmer – tennis-player etc. I am not flighty am I??!! You haven't given up hope for me yet have you?!! I really am serious-minded at times – I promise you!...

Baghdad   *10 January 1951*

'Now for Monday night...After a bit, there was a bang at the door and there was Ralph! He had hired a taxi – and was driving it himself which was rather fun. I jumped in and we drove down to the town talking hard all the way!...We went to the 'Tigris Palace Hotel' – one I have never been into, and it seemed terribly nice inside – better even than the 'Sindbad'. We went along to the bar first and had a sherry and talked. Then we had a most terrific dinner!! There was hors d'oevres, soup, fish, roast beef – and by that time I couldn't face what came next – steamed date pudding!! As Ralph couldn't either, we had fruit and finished there. He had brought a bottle of *lovely* red wine with him, which he said he had 'brought from foreign parts!!' Wasn't it fun?! I think he must have got it in Beirut, as he had flown there the day before – special for me!! He is terribly easy to talk to – and it really was *lovely* as we talked of interesting things without getting out of my depth – and it was terribly interesting. We discussed the problem of Iraqis etc. and the business of mixing with them – also learning Arabic etc. We also talked about Cyprus. He was stationed in the 'Dome Hotel' in the war, and just loves Cyprus. Anyway it was lovely and he made me feel perfectly at ease – didn't talk down to me at all – and I really felt I was quite intelligent! (very clever of him to make me even feel that!!).

We had to get to the Railway Club by 9.00 p.m. so we left pretty smartly, collected a driver, and drove over to the Club. It was terribly funny because all the rest of the Pilots' Mess (who always sit in the back row!) were all gaping and staring (even Neville) – however we got in alright – and who did I sit down next to but old Pat!! 'Hamlet' was just as good the second time – and didn't end till about 12.10 p.m. While we were waiting for the taxi we had another glass of wine!! He took me home, and when I was saying, 'thank you very much etc.' he was *frightfully* nice and said, 'I do hope you enjoyed it. Did you really enjoy it?' Then he said that we 'must do it again soon – *very* soon'!!! There – that's about the lot!!! It was so nice because he didn't kiss me or anything like that – I knew he wouldn't, and if he had I should have been very surprised – and rather disappointed. He really is terribly nice – and makes one feel so at ease. The wonderful part is that he is staying another *year*!!!! Isn't it grand?! Also, he has bought a car on the export and is expecting it to arrive any moment. I *did* enjoy myself terribly and do you think he *will* take me out again?…

Baghdad   *16 January 1951*

'...Derek...Came after supper and we talked for ages, and thrashed out my problem of Ralph!! Oh! dear! I do wish you were out here to talk to and get advice from. (This is a bit of a 'down' letter – by the way!!). Anyway, the whole thing is that ever since Monday, when he was so nice and said, 'We must do this again' etc. etc., I haven't seen him to speak to *once*! He has been playing tennis every day, but never stays to tea now, and I got it firmly fixed in my mind that he is trying to avoid me – and that by some awful chance he might think I am going to be another Jane Corner and chase him! This has worried me stiff for days, and if it hadn't been for Derek I don't know what I should do. Anyway, Derek came to dinner with me last night and we thrashed it all out! He is terribly reassuring and says that Ralph can't *possibly* think that, and that it is probably because he's shy or something, and is embarrassed when I'm with a whole crowd of people. It's logical enough, but I still can't quite be sure that he doesn't think I'm chasing him. Wouldn't it be *awful*?!! Derek says that he is positive it's alright, and that all I've got to do is to wait patiently. He thinks there are all sorts of reasons – one of them being that possibly he knows that I go around with Derek an awful lot – and thinks therefore that he's had his chips. Anyway, I've learnt my lesson and shan't confide in another soul except for Derek, as I'm sure it is a danger to tell one's girl friends! I have thought about it so much – what he's thinking I've thought he's thought etc. etc. – until I'm back where I started. However, I'm giving up worrying now – I can't do anything – except pin my faith on those words, 'we must do it again *very* soon!' What do you think about it all?...

I had a lift down to the 8.00 a.m. on Sunday with Bill Startup, but as he couldn't bring me back I walked over to the river, caught a bus down to Rashid Street, and then walked all the way back along the (bund) river bank as far as the club. It is about 2¹/₂ miles, but it was such a gorgeous morning, and hardly anybody about that I just loved it!! The river was all misty, and the sun was simply lovely. It really was a beautiful morning. By the time I reached the club I was ravenous, and so for a treat I thought I would treat myself to a Club breakfast!! My goodness – it was delicious. Eggs, bacon, mushrooms, toast and coffee!!! I did enjoy it…

(P.S. Was asked out by Sheikh Mohamed last night!! What *would* Col. Body say?! Declined, with thanks!).

Baghdad   *23 January 1951*

'…Oh! dear. Do you know I just *can't* stop thinking of Ralph. I have *never* been like this before!! It is a fortnight since I went out with him, and I haven't stopped thinking about him since!! However, not to worry unduly, as I am neither off my food nor getting noticeably thinner! I haven't even seen him since tennis last Sunday week, and I still have a horrible feeling that some-thing has happened and he is avoiding me. Derek still thinks it may be only shyness, but we both agree it is quite possible that some wretched person has gossiped (no uncommon occur-rence in B.) and it has got to his ears that 'Mary Borlase thinks she's hooked Ralph' – or something perfectly ghastly like that!!…It is all very disheartening and disappointing, and for once I don't mind from the 'glamour' point of view and what people will think etc., but I really do want him to go on liking me as I *know* he definitely was attracted. Anyway, never again do I indulge in 'girlish confidences' with my rather jealous (I'm afraid to say) friends such as Carol. Poor Carol, she certainly is jealous quite blatantly…At any rate I feel a lot wiser now, so if it all comes to nothing, I shall at least have learnt something out of my sad experiences!!! Oh! dear! Isn't life one big turmoil – but very exciting!…

Baghdad   *26 January 1951*

'Oh! It is so *cold*!! We had one degree of frost today…

By the way (at least – anything *but* 'by the way'). I think, hope and pray that things are going to be ALRIGHT after all!!! I saw Ralph yesterday for the first time for *ages*! Pat and I had been down the town having our polyphotos taken and came back to the Club for tea. I was sitting reading and heard Hamish say, 'Hullo Ralph' and there he was – scuttling straight through – but he came and stayed and talked and said that why hadn't Pat and I been playing tennis lately (that's good – as I was so afraid he might think I'd been going too often!! Anyway, we chatted away and he asked, 'How was I going to Arabic lessons?' – and in the end we all set off together (Pat too!). He suddenly asked if I was going to Ken's party! He is going – and I'm so thrilled as I never *dreamt* he'd be going to that sort of party. So now having been dreading it, I am now *dying* for tomorrow night!! We went out to the bus stop but in the end piled into a taxi, and I was dropped at the Iraqi Institute. It was terribly funny as he was sitting with his legs in the road, enquiring if I could get there etc. etc. alright, when the taxi started to proceed!! *ANYWAY*, I don't think anything has been wrong at all – and I think Derek is quite right and it is some form of shyness that has stopped him coming to tea! Gosh! So, I've had nearly three weeks' solid worry for nothing!!!! What a fool I am! Isn't life killing – up – down – up?!!…'

Baghdad   *30 January 1951*

'…Our new Ambassador, Sir John Troutbeck K.C.M.G., is married with two 'lush' daughters in their 20's!!! Anyway, he is reputed to be 'a very decent chap', and as we couldn't do much worse, I feel it will be a welcome change. They might have a few parties too with young offspring. Neville has often flown him from Cairo, and said he seems very nice.

The bomb episode didn't appear to cause a revolt or anything. It was all to do with this business of the evacuation of the Jews from Iraq. They are gradually being forced out of the country, and several hundreds leave each week. The ones who are still here have an awful time. We have some Jews in the next-door house, and there are always the most *appalling* rows going on as the owners of the house are trying to get rid of them.

'*Well*! I am feeling much better this week, and have decided to leave Ralph to stew in his own horrible lonely juice!! The last straw was on Saturday morning when Kenneth suddenly said that Ralph couldn't come to his party!! I was simply furious and bitterly disappointed. I had a lovely little moan to myself all afternoon, thought things over, and gradually came to my senses – again! I decided he was a horrible self-centred prig anyway, and a complete introvert!! He is *always* refusing Ken's invitations – and I am quite sure he hasn't always got another engagement! He loathes parties anyway, and is a bit *too* anti-social for my liking!! He goes to the other extreme. So what we want is the happy medium. (Neville?!!!). Anyway, I really thought a lot about it and it was amazing how sensible I became all at once. There are 'more fish in the sea' anyway, and it's no good going around moping as one would look a bit of a fool. Anyway, I went off to Ken's party full of renewed vigour, and to my surprise thoroughly enjoyed myself! I can't think how Ralph would have fitted in to the general set-up, so it was just as well he wasn't there. There were about 20 of us and I must admit if it hadn't been for Johnny's and Neville's saving presence I probably should have loathed it!…Neville…stayed and was *terribly* nice. Isabel and Jack decided to depart about 2.30 and I'd had enough by then too. So Neville said he would see me safely home – and as it was only just round the corner, we walked. He was very nice, and dropped his facetiousness at once – and the first thing he said as we walked down the road was, 'What a change it was to see a fresh English face like mine'. Wasn't that nice? So I feel my future success definitely lies in remaining a 'fresh English girl' – unspoilt and rosy-cheeked (?!) etc. etc. I think *however* fascinated people appear to be by Pat Comber and her highly amusing songs etc., they still appreciate a real English girl!! Anyway he came in for a moment, and then suddenly kissed me. He *was* so nice – and said I had a nice cool cheek – then Isabel and Jack rolled up in the car! But it was nice, and so I don't think I've fallen for Ralph any more than I've ever fallen for anyone *yet*! (Actually its only the second person who has kissed me properly – Derek being the first). The awful people like Perry Fellowes don't count!!…

Yesterday was bank day and, believe it or not, when I walked into the Ottoman Bank a complete stranger (Iraqi) came up and said, 'Hullo, Miss Mary', and then proceeded to ask for my phone number as his sister wanted to meet me. Gosh! I was *livid*! It really is a bit much – and I am sick to death of those people – what with Nuri Faiq, Sheikh Mohamed etc. etc., I feel like a mouse in a trap being pursued all round the place. I am fast running out of excuses too! What a life!…'

Baghdad   *6 February 1951*

'…Oh! I must tell you – my 'thermometer' has risen with a bang again!! On Sunday morning just as we were getting ready for the lunch party, Ralph rang up (he must know us!) and asked me to play tennis that afternoon. I explained that I didn't think I'd be able to get rid of my guests in time; so we fixed for today. I *was* surprised though – as I thought ALL was over. I have just rung up now to confirm that it is off for this afternoon. I got Johnny first, who went to get Ralph. When

Ralph started speaking there were most extraordinary roaring noises – which turned out to be Johnny! We decided it was too wet…and so now we are playing on Friday! We (Isabel and I) have been trying to fix up this 'intellectual' dinner party for ages – and so I asked Ralph if he could come on Friday – and he leapt at it. So *that's* alright. Now we must collect some other bodies!!…In the course of conversation, Ralph said that *Neville* sent his love to me – so what with Johnny's noises off and one thing and other it was quite hilarious!!!…I dreamt about Ralph and Neville the other night – what a muddle!!!! Anyway, I think they are both *GORGEOUS* and very nice…'

Baghdad   *9 February 1951*

'I had a lovely game of tennis with Ralph. We played three sets which he won 6-2, 6-2, 6-1!! After that we knocked up and he told me all the things I wasn't doing right! So really it was *terribly* nice – and very good for me…

Pauline and Michael are back, and Isabel and I plucked up all our courage and dashed round to see them yesterday evening. Pauline looks alright – but rather tired – big circles round her eyes – but otherwise they seemed to be alright!…

Our dinner party…All went off very well we thought, and the dinner was good and there was lots to drink. Isabel had bought some green chartreuse at the NAAFI, which was very popular. We had some terribly interesting conversations – and oh! what a change to hear people talking sensibly and seriously. It really was a joy – as they were all of an intellectual turn of mind and it was such a relief after the endless 'party chatter' that one gets so sick of. Ralph and Isabel had some very deep debate about religion – which I just managed to understand without my dictionary! Anyway we talked and talked and they didn't leave until 11.00 p.m. Ralph is going to give me an Airways calendar – with magnificent pictures of New York etc.

It will be rather nice for the office. He was *terribly* nice yesterday – and we had some awfully interesting talks about this and that. He is quite interested in music and always used to go to the British Institute concerts etc.

(My goodness!! I have just had the shock of my life!! The Iraq Times has just come in, and I was just having a quick 'go-through' it before giving it to Kenneth – when I turned it over and saw *me* – large as life on the back page!! It is a photo of the fancy-dress dance – and of course of all the 300-odd they took – they *would* choose the one of me dancing with old wet-blob Gussie pants – and looking *dreadful* – for the whole of Iraq to see!!! *Misery* – I shall never live this down!!!!)'…

Baghdad   *13 February 1951*

'…Last night Isabel and I…Went down to the British Institute to hear the concert. It was given by the Padre (piano) and Sandu Albu (violin) and one of the latter's pupils – Vartan Manoogian (an Armenian) who played second violin…I believe Armenians are very musical as a rule. It was rather fun after, as several of us had drinks, and met all sorts of interesting people. I talked to the Albus who are Hungarian I think…I have made a resolution to go *every* Monday again to the gramophone concerts…

I have quite decided that *if* I ever get married I *must* marry someone with intellectual inclinations. Life would be *so* much more interesting, and Isabel quite agrees. She is always saying that if you had to be wrecked on a desert island for 50 years, it would be much better to be with somebody intellectual and clever and amusing like Philip Mallet or Ralph!…

…Our interpreter – Hanna Azar al Banna – has just invited us to the wedding of his eldest son – Fuad – to an English girl called Sheila Moses. Fuad met her when he was training at Southampton with the R.A.F. and she is coming out to marry him on Friday. We have all (Rays, etc.) been invited to the wedding which is at 5.00 p.m. at the Protestant Church. Then they are having a reception at the Railway Club from 6.00 p.m. – 8.00 p.m.

Baghdad   *21 February 1951*

'…The wedding…*Was* an experience, and I wouldn't have missed it for the world!! It was held in the Protestant Church, which is rather like a village hall, although it has an altar, harmonium etc. Anyway, Isabel and I sat there, our noses being tickled by a palm leaf, and waited for the service to begin! It was taken both in English and Arabic by two priests (who sat with their backs to the altar), but otherwise it more or less seemed to follow the normal marriage service. They, of course, had their responses in English. It was late in starting and the noise was dreadful – cars hooting outside – and people walking in the whole way through. I thought the girl bore up to it all amazingly well. There must have been nearly 20 bridesmaids of varying shapes, sizes and breeds (all relatives of course!) and we sang one hymn. As it was in Arabic, Isabel and I could do no more than hum the tune which, amazingly enough, was 'John Brown's Body'!!! We got a lift down to the Railway Club and there of course had to wait for *hours*! The ballroom was reserved for the reception and everyone sat at little tables, there being a large space in the middle. There was even a band – the Apollo Band – and the cake (five tiers!!) was placed on a table in the centre of the room. Nothing happened for about half an hour, and Isabel and I just sat getting more and more bored. Then the Chief Pilot, Tom Walters and his wife, came in and we giggled at them across the room. Suddenly the band struck up the Wedding March and we all got excited, but it was a false alarm! However, a few minutes later they tried again – and in came the bride and bridegroom and we all stood up and clapped!! They sat in two armchairs facing us all. Then after a minute they proceeded to cut the cake, accompanied by suitable chords from the Apollo Band!! We all clapped again – and then the champagne came round followed by enormous chunks of cake. Philip Ray slipped in and joined us at this stage. The next thing that happened was that the band suddenly broke into the dance tune, 'I'll be loving you – always' and (believe it or not!) the bride and bridegroom proceeded to do a solo dance! What an ordeal – and I'm thankful it isn't a normal British custom – she was trying to negotiate her long wedding dress too!! After their little exhibition the floor seemed to be open to all! Johnny and Ralph rolled up next, and Ralph said I must have a dance later – when a few more people had started! So I had my dance with him – and then Neville rolled up…

Baghdad   *27 February 1951*

'…One funny incident was when Max Reynolds came up to me and said, 'Is it true you're engaged?!' This was really most exciting, but he wouldn't disclose who I was engaged to – which was rather tantalising! Perhaps he has been looking at certain photographs in photographers' shops!!! Isn't it amazing how stories get around out here?! The other funny thing was that Mr Gauntlett came up to me (the Consul) and said he'd heard I'd been troubled by mysterious phone calls etc. and was being pursued around the place! Anyway, he'd been hearing the most blood-curdling stories and was ready to bring all H.B.M.'s power into action. However, I assured him that all was well, and things had a way of getting exaggerated!…

…I got a lift down the town in the Embassy car as far as the Museum (which I have been meaning to visit for ages). I went round all alone and must have spent nearly two hours there. It was really enthralling and I looked at old stones and pottery etc. from about 5,000 B.C. up to the time of the country being defeated by the Moslems in about 300 or so A.D. I saw all the old Sumerian stuff, Babylonian and Assyrian. It was all beautifully tabulated and easy to follow. I also had a book of Isabel's which helped. When I got back home in the afternoon I read up the brief outline of history for that time, made notes, and have really got it all tabulated now! Isn't it interesting though, there seemed to be nothing but wars with first one city state and then another holding supremacy over the others. However, I have sorted out the ancient Assyrian capitals, when Babylon was capital, when it was destroyed etc., and also names such as Sennacherib, Ashurbanipal etc., all make sense now…

…I also went into the suq on Sunday morning and pottered along. The Coppersmith's Bazaar really is a picture! I visited Hassan Halabi who is the Persian dealer and I bought a little Persian picture which I thought you might like for Easter…I really rather like the Persian art. I asked the prices of all sorts of things – with an eye on the future! I really must collect some nice things before I go home…

P.S…No, I certainly see now that parties aren't the sole joys of life, and am quite determined to pursue my 'intellectual and artistic' amusements! There is so much to be got out of life, and I just can't imagine how people can ever be bored or wonder what to do with themselves, can you? There is so much to learn – it is almost discouraging at times. I sometimes wonder just what one learns at school?!'…

Baghdad   *2 March 1951*

'Oh! dear! I'm feeling ever so feek and weable, as it was the Caledonian Ball last night, and I have only had about 3½ hours sleep!…It was my first experience of a proper Caledonian Ball, and I must say I thoroughly enjoyed it. But – oh! – horrors – Athol Brose!! Have you ever tasted anything quite so revolting in your life? It looks and tastes just like Milk of Magnesia with a flavouring of porridge! However, I must start at the beginning. Derek collected me about 8.00 p.m. and we went to their house and had drinks before going on to the dance at about 9.30 p.m…We arrived at the dance and Jimmy presented us all to the President – Mrs Garbutt. The place was very nicely decorated, and all round the walls of the dance floor they had draped different tartan plaids – with a little note to say which clan they were. There were some lovely ones – and they even had a McKenzie! They had the Stuart, Gordon, Lord of the Isles, and simply heaps more. The first thing that happened was this revolting Athol Brose – Ugh! However, Derek drank mine! My dear! We actually had dance programmes!! It is the first time I have ever been to a dance where they've had them before. I must admit they were rather fun, but full of snags and disadvantages! I am very glad I didn't live in Victorian days. I did most of the Scottish dances with Derek which was nice. The dancing started off with a grand march. We marched off in twos, and then split up into fours, and finally eights, and then we started off with an eightsome reel. We had two straight off, and I was just dripping! The next Scottish one was the Dashing White Sergeant, which I did with Derek and Jimmy. That is a lovely one, but also very hot-making! Then we had Strip the Willow, and the buffet supper started at midnight. I had worked up quite an appetite by then, in spite of having demolished two (small!) boiled eggs, toast and coffee at 6.30! The Padre was at the dance, and also the R.A.F. Padre from Habbaniya – and they were most amusing. There were certainly a lot of people there, and it was a great success. The Stuart-Williamses were there, and Guss-pants, with their usual set of empty-headed friends! Max Reynolds danced the entire evening (at these big public dances) with Frances Dinwiddie, who is the empty-headed, flitter-pated wife of quite a nice man. Anyway, they just make me SICK – and all that set seem to enjoy nothing but chasing each other's husbands. Oh! I think it's dreadful! Still, I suppose it all comes from having not enough to do and general boredom and lack of education. (This latter at least seems to provide people with the ability and impetus to be able to find their own amusements and interests). To leave that sordid subject! However, it makes Derek and most decent people feel slightly sick too, so I am not the only one! In the last half we had another eightsome, and Petronella. We also did the Gay Gordons (which I had never done before!). It is an absolute beauty – terribly easy – but it looks very graceful and nice. I did that with Derek, and also the Schottishe which I have just about mastered. They *are* fun these Scottish dances, and now that I have got the hang of them, they seem much easier and less alarming!…The dance ended about 2.45 a.m. with Auld Lang Syne etc., and I suppose I was in bed by about 3.20'…

Baghdad   *6 March 1951*

'On Saturday we both went down to the British Institute to hear the lecture [by Professor Mallowan] on Nimrud. Of course, I found myself sitting just behind Agatha [Christie], so I couldn't make my usual comments throughout!! He gave quite a good talk, explaining latern slides as he showed them on the screen. However, both Isabel and I felt that he made an enthralling subject extremely dull. He didn't really tell us the interesting bits about the history of the place, etc., but only rather technical details of how many tons of earth had to be sifted – which isn't all that interesting to the layman. However, it was most amusing at the end, as the (Iraqi) Director of Anti-quities stood up to give the Vote of Thanks. His speech lasted nearly as long as the lecture – was read, rather stumblingly, word for word, and contained the most wonderful aphorisms, platitudes, perorations etc. I couldn't help a snigger when he referred to the 'wonderful work of Professor Mallowan, who with his *artful* hands gave us so many wonderful prizes etc.'…

On Sunday morning I went down to the town by bus and visited the other museum…It deals almost entirely with the Islamic Period – from about the 9th Century A.D. onwards till about 1500 A.D. There were some very fine old doors carved or inlaid most beautifully, which were excavated from Samarra, about 1300 A.D. They also had some beautifully decorated copies of the Quran'…

Baghdad   *9 March 1951*

'I have just had a lift home on…? Yes – a motor bike!! I can't *think* who owns a motor bike, can you?!!! I hadn't seen Ralph for ages until this afternoon. I went down to the club to have a game…I then had a shower, changed, and had tea on the lawn and read my book. After a bit Ralph appeared and joined me for tea – wasn't that nice?!! We chatted away – and he knows Netheravon and loves Salisbury. He, by the way, lives in Epsom! He is going to the Mozart concert tonight too, so we shall see him there. Then he offered me a lift home on the motor bike. It *was* fun!! So now I feel on top of the world again – not that I was down before!'…

Baghdad   *14 March 1951*

'…There is a wholesale persecution of the Jews going on in Baghdad now, and they really are having a dreadful time. Some time ago, as you will know, the Iraq Government issued the ultimatum that all Jews were either to accept Iraqi nationality for life – or get out! Of course thousands and thousands registered to go, but although a tremendous number have already gone, it still leaves a large number waiting to go. It is these unfortunates upon whom the Government have just descended. The banks were closed on Saturday, and all the Jews' 'assets' are being frozen – and confiscated. Yesterday they were holding up cars, and if you happened to be a Jew you got out and walked and your car was there and then confiscated. They are confiscating their houses, property, and in fact anything that can be turned into ready cash. If you employ a Jew he can't be paid, but you pay his salary to the newly set up Controller in the Government. So the Government is taking everything, and intends to give each Jew an allowance to live on until they leave the country. Isn't it *dreadful*? Of course, it is causing chaos as there are masses of Jews in high positions in banks, R.O.C., and ordinary offices etc., who are all dismissed, with the result that the banks etc., are pretty under-staffed. Yesterday in the cloth bazaar apparently, the Jews were selling cotton for about 2/- an enormous bale – or just flinging it down for a few fils. Now would be the time to pick up things cheap, but of course it is illegal as the Government is confiscating everything. I can't help thinking some people's pockets are going to be very comfortably lined. Isn't it dreadful though – to think of having even one's furniture and personal belongings confiscated?…

The Iraqi party on Monday night, which I was dreading so, went off alright and wasn't at all bad. Bill Creech didn't collect me until 9.40 p.m. and so I was beginning to feel hungry (nothing since tea!) and sleepy! However, I had steeled myself to be 'diplomatic' *all* evening, with the result that I really did quite enjoy it. It was a party of about 30 and we sat round a dinner table shaped like an E without the central stroke. We danced non-stop before the cabaret started, and by 11.30 I had talked my head off, and danced my feet off!! I was seated between the nice Sheikh Mohamed (not a word to Col. Body!!!) and some foreign office official. We didn't have dinner until 11.40 but I had been kept going by the formidable array of cutlery etc. in front of me. We had soup, then fish, and then chicken and rice (the latter I concluded to be the main course!). However, next came meat and vegetables etc. etc.! Then there was a lull – and the cabaret had by this time finished – and we danced again. I thought that was the end – so powdered my nose etc., only to find on my return a plate of sweet!!! We then had fruit and coffee! However, my success (or rather well-being next day!) lay in the fact that I had only *one* drink the entire evening. I met an Iraqi captain who had been stationed with the School of Infantry at Warminster, and that common bond seemed most amusing! Even more amusing (?) when he informed me that the other three Iraqis he had been there with had *all* married English girls. He was the only unlucky one?!! I extricated myself from this unhappy story and returned to deal (highly satisfactorily and diplomatically!) with Sheikh Mohamed. He is, I gather, a highly respected Member of Parliament and the best sheikh for miles around. He has fair hair and wears European clothes, and is a *highly* intelligent man…At any rate he extended many invitations and I was beginning to get slightly perturbed when I remembered I had seen him at the hotel when I went with Ralph! So gradually (and diplomatically) I began bringing 'my friend' (no names) into the conversation and mentioning riding on the back of motorbikes as if it was a daily habit! I told him all about the little M.G. even – and then he said (as I'd hoped), 'Is your friend the same as I saw you with in the hotel?' And so with perfect truthfulness and shining eyes (!) I was able to say, 'Yes'!!! All this went down very well – and he even said that I looked far away (at one silent moment on my part – rare), as though I was sitting in the little M.G.!!!'…

Baghdad   *20 March 1951*

'Isn't the Persian situation grim?! I certainly don't fancy going there just now!!! Yesterday a bomb was thrown at the American Information Office in Baghdad – and I gather several people were hurt but none killed!! Never a dull moment is there?!!! Derek says if someone throws a bomb at you, the thing to do is pick it up and hurl it back before it has had time to explode!! However, most of them only have an 8-second time-lag, so I don't think I should get far!!!...The oil situation is very serious and I have been talking to masses of people about it. We should just *have* to defend Abadan, I think, as oil goes from there to the entire world. 40% of the oil from Persia goes to America, so they too will want to keep it. I just don't know what is going to happen – but of course if the Persians are allowed to run their own show, it wouldn't be long before Russia stepped in to assist!! Then – as far as I can see – (my own opinion!) we should be doomed as without *any* supplies from Persia we should have to bargain and give in to whatever Russia asks. Still – I don't imagine England or America will sit back and allow that to happen...

...I was asked out to dinner by a man called James Norton. He is a travelling agent for Dunlop tyres or something – and stays in Baghdad for about a week every three months or so...He is a nice man – about 29 – 34 or so. Anyway, we went to the Semiramis Hotel for dinner and there joined Maureen who was having dinner with a nice B.O.A.C. representative she had met in Bahrain. We had a *very* pleasant evening...He has asked me to dinner again on Wednesday – and I have accepted...He is quite a nice young man – rather silly – but just the type who has a 'girl in every port' I should imagine!...Isn't it amazing? A few months ago I should have been madly thrilled by it all – and now it doesn't worry me. I am learning to discriminate at last!!! Still – I *must* snap out of Ralph soon – or I shall get quite worried!!! Amazing – it's lasted nearly four months now!!!...

★   ★   ★

CHAPTER 7

Baghdad
31.03.51 - 23.06.51

Easter Monday 1951

'...I went to the hotel after and met James Norton (Dunlop) who I was having dinner with. We had a drink in his room first (rather improper?!) and then the most *excellent* dinner – starting off with caviar! He is a nice young man – ex-Marlburian – aged 33...We talked and talked and he announced he was staying till Monday and would I have dinner again etc. etc. He was most insistent, but I am afraid I was very discouraging and said I couldn't!...He is quite harmless, but I'm just not madly struck, so I don't think it is much good leading him on, do you?...

The Rays collected me about 12 or so, and we went off to Ctesiphon. It is a lovely run of about 15 miles, and we crossed over the Diyala – a tributary of the Tigris – on the way...We had our picnic lunch in a date-grove near the River, a little way away from Ctesiphon...Then we ended up by going over to see the arch of Ctesiphon itself. It is the most amazing piece of architecture – and is the largest unsupported arch in the world!!! Ctesiphon was the capital of the Parthians in about 200 B.C. an so the arch is about 2,000 years old. It really is an impressive sight! We got back for tea...

Yesterday...We were able to go on our picnic...We went down the Babylon road for a few miles, and then got down to the river and picnicked at a place called Dora! It wasn't very hot, but really very nice. I am just *praying* that my films will come out, as there were some really quite interesting ones. A man came along in a tiny hand-made canoe and held up two *enormous* fish he had speared!! So I photographed him – and then the hunt passed – all in pink coats. I have never seen them before – and it was funny to see the Arab head-dresses with pink coats underneath! The next excitement was an enormous paddle-steamer passing on its way down to Basra! I believe they are practically extinct and that special type with stern paddles a great rarity!! So I photographed madly! We also saw a gufa and it really was a fascinating party!!…

Baghdad   *31 March 1951*

'…Isn't it lucky it's not Ralph that is leaving so soon? I really don't know what I should do if he was going – as it gives me a tremendous zest for life! When I've seen him, or had tea with him or something, it carries me on for days in absolute bliss!! I don't mean from a sentimental point of view – but from an ordinary 'interest' point of view. Oh! dear. I can't quite explain what I mean – but after I've been talking to him for a bit, I am filled with all the marvellous things there are to do in life, and all that there is to *learn*. It is most stimulating – intellectually, I mean! — mentally alert – that's what he makes one! You suddenly appreciated *everything* – weather, flowers, birds, art, music – and ad infinitum!! Jolly Good Thing.

Baghdad   *1 April 1951*

'…Derek departed [on leave] on Saturday evening by Nairn. Now he will be in Beirut. Poor thing – he was *frightfully* het up about the whole thing. I had dinner with him on Friday night – and apparently the trouble is that there is an ex-bomber pilot on the spot – with a car and pots of money – and I gather he is turning on the pressure and poor old Ann doesn't know where she is. As Derek says, she is *very* honest, and tells him all – and so he feels that this fortnight will either make or finish him. I just pray everything will be alright. Poor Derek – he really went off looking almost ill with worry and apprehension. If he comes back an engaged man, it is going to be extremely amusing from my point of view, because although a lot of people know all about Ann etc., there are still *masses* to whom it must look as though I am the object of his attentions etc. I expect people will be eyeing me with apprehension – and expecting me to die of a broken heart!!! Still – *we* understand each other, – and that's all that matters. All the same I miss Derek – it doesn't seem the same without him.

However, my day was made on Saturday by the most *gorgeous* letter from Michael [Clapp]. Oh! I *do* like him, Mummy. Isn't it fun – that he is growing up too? We both agree that going abroad is marvellous – and the only thing. He said in his letter that he noticed the girls in jobs at home were all rather dull – and 'easily shocked'. It was a 10-side letter – and very interesting!'…

Baghdad   *7 April 1951*

'…Isabel and I are going to give a dinner party next Friday, and I thought I'd ask Ralph again – because I'd had to refuse him three times!! So I plucked up my courage and rang up on Wednesday night. I think I must have got 'Nobby' first, but then Ralph came and said, 'Hullo', and then these awful tin tray noises started up again. Ralph disappeared and then came back saying it was Neville! However, everything quietened down after a bit. That Mess is just like a menagerie!! I was quite prepared for Ralph to refuse this time, but when I said would he like to come to dinner next week, he said he'd just love to!! So that was encouraging. Then – my goodness – we must have talked for a good twenty minutes!!…

I had a terrific argument with Mrs Sallis at dinner (friendly)

over whether or not it was a good thing I was out here. She says
I am too young, and will get disillusioned etc. But I just don't
agree – and think I have learnt much more by seeing other
people who *are* disillusioned etc. and fed up with life. I have
learnt so many lessons about other people's mistakes etc. too.
But she has very odd ideas over lots of things – and is a great
friend of Mrs Sworder's, so I don't think her opinions are going
to bother me. Blow me if the subject of Ralph didn't come up
again at dinner. Mrs Sallis says she thinks he is very nice.
Anyway, they went on about it – and I sat silent! (Ha! Ha!)'…

Baghdad   *11 April 1951*

'…On Sunday afternoon the Indonesian boy came along and
took me for my first driving lesson! My dear! Isn't it easy?! I
just couldn't believe it – and do you know I even found I could
still TALK!! Of course, I imagine that a Buick like that is far
easier to drive than most English cars. We went out along the
Baquba road which is pretty deserted, and so we only met one
or two cars. I nearly ran over a dog as I hadn't yet learnt to stop,
but all was well! I was terribly good at starting without a terrific
bump and a shoot forward. By the end we were starting off
most beautifully smoothly! I did enjoy it'.

Baghdad   *14 April 1951*

'Tremendous excitement, relief etc. Derek has just rung up
and he has got engaged!! Isn't it simply marvellous?! I just had
to write and tell you at once!! He got back on the Nairn this
morning and Isabel answered the 'phone. I asked him how he
was, and was very relieved to hear he was 'bursting with
health'. Then he said he'd also got engaged…I am just so
thrilled for Derek, and was absolutely terrified he'd come back
unengaged and drink himself to death or something awful!…

…Then we walked round to Bob's house. It was really a very nice party – masses of Americans but also Philip Mallet and John Cloake and another Hollway Bros. Man called 'Henry' from the Railway Club. We had a most delicious supper – danced – and did one or two reels. There were only four of us who could do them – so we showed off like mad!! I was complimented on my dancing – and told HOW LIGHT I WAS ON MY FEET!!!…My dear! – Philip Mallet was quite drunk (in a nice way) and even John Cloake was most unrestrained! I was dancing with Philip and then we sat on a sofa and he put his arm round me! I was so embarrassed – as it is most unlike Philip. Then he took me home in the Flying Bomb – he was so funny as he kept apologising and saying he had drunk too much!!'…

Baghdad   *19 April 1951*

'…Who should be in church on Sunday night but 'Dunlop' back again from his travels!! He came up after and asked me to dinner but added that his boss was with him as well! Anyway I couldn't really stay to dinner as Bakr was doing a hot dinner specially for us, and Isabel had already accepted a dinner invitation, so I said I couldn't really manage it. Blow me, if a dreadful woman called Mrs Hynd didn't overhear this and come up (interfering old hussy!) and say I mustn't refuse a good offer like that etc. etc. I was simply livid. Aren't people awful?! Anyway, 'Dunlop' hadn't got his car, so Mrs Pearce gave him, and Arnold Crow, and myself all a lift back and we went in for a drink with 'Dunlop' at the Semiramis Hotel. He said he must fetch his boss, as 'he might feel left out'. He was rather a nice old boy, and came pottering along saying he was forever having to come down and drink!! 'Dunlop' announced that he would have to be coming to Baghdad a lot this summer because of the Jewish business etc., and he asked if I was going

to be here all summer. When I said that I was he announced
that it would make Baghdad more exciting. But from the way
he said it I couldn't make out if it was making Baghdad more
exciting for me having him popping down every now and
again, or vice-versa!! He asked if I knew the Sauders, and then
said they were having them to dinner on Wednesday night, and
would I like to come too. I really felt I couldn't face Mrs
Sworder (correct spelling this time!) drooling and slobbering
all evening. So I said I wasn't really sure that I could manage it.
He said he would ring up sometime, but I was really quite
relieved that I heard nothing and they have left for Beirut
today. A Good Thing!…

Baghdad   *21 April 1951*

'…The Embassy Cocktail Party last night was tremendous
fun! I found myself chatting away to Lady Troutbeck at one
stage in the evening, just as if she was my aunt or something!
The Rays collected Isabel and me – and the flap we were all in
about our hats etc. It was too funny! Bridget looked terribly
sweet, in a pretty flowered dress with a 'hat' of real verbena
sewn onto a black ribbon. It was made at the last minute and
really looked excellent!! We arrived slightly early over the other
side, and so Philip drove us all round the railway compound
first. Then we arrived, and there was a frantic powdering of
noses, straightening of stocking seams etc, and then in we
marched. It is the first time I have ever been inside the
residential part of the Embassy – and it really is most imposing.
In the hall there is a real goldfish pond (tiled) with a fountain
in the middle. I was warned not to fall into it, as the French
Minister apparently did the other day! I did get away without
falling into it, but just as I was passing it on my way out, my
pearls broke and one bounced away into the water!! Bridget
was marvellous and dived into the water (only her arm!) and

fished it out! Trust me to do something – but at any rate I didn't upset any glasses or anything. As we went into the drawing room at the beginning we were all introduced to H.E. and Lady Troutbeck by John Cloake, and then we just stood around. I talked to all sorts of people, and met some awfully nice girls up from Kuwait. One, especially nice, was an Australian girl who is a nursing sister at the Kuwait Oil company hospital. She hasn't been there very long and was thrilled to hear all about Cyprus, where she is going for leave in September. She was terribly lively, with a tremendous zest for life and interest in everything. We did a rapid exchange of names etc. in case she ever gets to Baghdad again! H.E. and Lady T. were simply marvellous and must have got round to speak to nearly everyone – which is a vast improvement on the Macks, who apparently used to just stand surrounded by the Counsellor and First Secretary for the entire evening. Anyway, Lady T. came up to me and asked how long I had been here etc, etc. She was very interested in the job and her younger daughter is now doing secretarial training in London. She isn't coming out here, I gather, unless she has a job. She said that I was a very good advertisement for Baghdad, as I looked so well! I felt I must remember that and tell you!! By the way – I wore my little blue again and am really quite attached to it by now! It was much admired so I take back all of my remarks about making me buy it – what a waste etc. etc. Mummy, dear – you are *always* right!!! (Oh! while I remember – I feel this is an opportune moment to ask if you could possibly send me one or two more tins of Amm-I-Dent tooth powder?!!)'…

Baghdad   *27 April 1951*

'…My dear! I hardly dare tell you. We have had a rise in our Foreign Service Allowance!!! It's all Miss Weldsmith's doing – dear soul. Now this is *strictly confidential* (for you and Daddy only) as it is meant to be a state secret anyway – our pay! We now get £525 p.a. F.S.A. in addition to our ordinary pay of £260 p.a. or whatever it is. So here am I at the age of 20 earning approximately £750 p.a. free of Income Tax!!! Actually there is a sting in it, as we now have to pay all electricity, water, heating, paraffin etc. bills. But I still think it will make a stupendous difference, and mean Isabel and I won't have to exist on a piece of lettuce for the last week of each month! However, I am absolutely determined to *save* and *save*, as I know that never in my life will I have so much money again!...

...We went down to the cinema after dinner and really thoroughly enjoyed it. There was an awful moment though, when a strange man clutched me!! I was sitting on Ralph's left – and there was a row of empty seats on my left. A man who had been sitting at the far end suddenly moved up to one away from me, as I thought so he could see better! However, just at an amusing moment in the film when we were all lurching about in our seats I felt an awful clutch on my leg – I clutched Ralph (who obviously thought I'd gone mad) and hissed in his ear! He was pretty quick in the uptake and we just swapped over seats in an instant – and then the offending man just walked off – so all was well! Wasn't it horrid though? I was glad I wasn't alone...Anyway, it was a lovely evening and I *loved* every minute of it. Ralph brought me back, saying he was going to bring back the most gorgeous wines from Italy etc. etc...

Now, Mummy, *do* be enthusiastic! Do you know my first thought when I went upstairs was to dash into your bedroom and tell you all – just as I used to do at home after dances!! Oh! I do miss you, and wish you were here to share my enthusiasms etc. Life is certainly 'rose-tinted' at the moment – and long may it last. But you aren't disapproving or anything are you? You just don't seem *quite* as enthusiastic and pleased as usual – but perhaps that's natural in a letter. But if you only knew how nice Ralph was – honestly, I'm sure you'd be just as excited as me. You aren't afraid I'd get *engaged* to him or anything are you?! Because don't for a moment worry about that! I am *quite* sure he wouldn't ever even think of anything like that. It is a purely platonic friendship, and that is what I like about him. So different from people like 'Dunlop' who are embarrassingly fast – always trying to kiss one. HORRIBLE!! So please don't think anything of it, or take me any more seriously than usual!!…

Ralph is going [on leave] for a month, so I suppose he will be back at the beginning of June. In the meantime our new girl (described as 'older and quieter') arrives, and we will be getting her introduced and settled in'…

Baghdad   *30 April 1951*

'…On Friday evening…we went on to hear the Baghdad Symphony Orchestra's concert. Quite an experience!! They started with a Bach suite which wasn't too good – and they had to stop at one point and start again as half the orchestra repeated and half didn't!! That was just strings, but the next item – a Mozart symphony – was *full* orchestra! The conductor (Albu) nearly fell of the rostrum in his excitement and rage. Being in the front row we had the full blast of his hisses, 'pom, pom, pom' etc. etc.!! The features of some of the players were a wonderful sight, but it wasn't awfully good. However, after the interval they seemed to get more confident and played a difficult Tchaikowsky serenade really *very* well indeed. The last item was a Chopin piano concerto which was good, as Hertz 'carried' it entirely at the piano. But on the whole it was a good effort when you think that very few of the orchestra have ever seen any good symphony orchestras. Quite a thing though, in later years, to be able to say, 'Oh, yes, I once heard the Baghdad Symphony Orchestra play that, my dear, back in 1951'…

Ralph said wouldn't I stay for a drink and have dinner?...
Then started the first of Ralph's, 'Oh! I've forgotten to do...'!!!
Apparently he was meant to have met his Jewish Arabic-teacher
at a café on the bund to say goodbye, as the man is off to Israel.
So in the end we both went along the bund, found the café,
and sat down and had a Coca-Cola. It *was* fun, and the first
time I've been in a proper Arab café overlooking the Tigris in
the moonlight. It really did look lovely – and all along the shore
were bright fires where 'masquf' was being cooked. It was nice
and cool outside too, and great fun. The teacher turned up and
was promptly dreadfully embarrassed as he thought he'd
interrupted us!!! However, we reassured him and he came and
sat down and talked. It is pathetic, as he is off to Israel this
week, having never left Baghdad in his life! He has no idea
even what happens to him when he gets off the plane at Lydda.
It must be *awful*'...

Baghdad   *4 May 1951*

'...Isabel and I are planning to go to Mosul for Whitsun...
Nigel Power very kindly is fixing up with the Consul and his
wife, to see if we can be put up. We get Monday off anyway, so
it is a great chance for Isabel and I to go together without
missing any work...

Oh! I get so excited when I think about it all – but still I keep
telling myself to be sensible. I think it is quite a good thing
really – and I *may* by the end of the month find I don't really
miss Ralph at all. (I can't believe it now – but you never
know!!!). He is so nice – and best of all – so unlike those
ordinary 'Dunlops' etc. and the usual fast types! Oh! Gosh! I
mustn't go off again or I shall be on another page before I
know where I am. But *AIN'T LIFE JUST FUN*!!!?

Baghdad   *15 May 1951*

'...the Music Festival...The music went off excellently until the last item...We sang 'The heavens are telling'. It is a lovely noisy cheerful thing – and Pat and I got so carried away we missed our lead completely, lost the place, and didn't find it again until nearly the end!! The funny thing was we thought we had found it and started singing lustily, only to find we hadn't got to that part yet!!! However, it wasn't *entirely* our fault as the tenors (who we follow) had missed their lead in the first place! After all that it was very comforting to find that a fair proportion of the congregation hadn't noticed anything wrong!

We had a terrific buffet supper in the Padre's garden after – with the Iraq Army Band playing in the background. It would have been a delightful evening if only we had been able to *sit* down somewhere. By 10.00 p.m. we were all drooping against trees etc. and Lady Troutbeck was sitting on the verandah steps! The Bishop was there – and I went up and spoke to him as he was all alone! As far as I can remember he only told me what he'd had for lunch!! Then of course I did a thing I've *never* done before – I left my comb and lipstick in the Very Rev. the Lord Bishop of Jerusalem's bedchamber!!!! I'd been washing etc. and then shot off into the first likely looking bedroom to do my hair – and left my things!! I didn't realise till next morning – and the Padre was awfully hassled and said the Bishop had popped out of his room saying, '*Whose* are these?'...

We arrived at Mosul at 7.00 a.m. and they had sent the driver and car to meet us and take us to the Consulate. It is a fascinating building – looking quite old as it has lovely battlements! The Union Jack (an extra large one for Sundays!) looked most impressive...The 'family' consist (at present!) of Alec Sinclair (Vice-Consul) who is a broad Scots and terribly nice – and Evelyn, his Canadian wife, and daughter Mary aged 19 months and another expected during the next month!!

Anyway they were dears and made us feel perfectly at home...Then, Tony Collier rang up. So we arranged to go over to his house at 10.30. There were just four of us, Tony, Robin, Isabel and myself – and we went to a lovely spot called Min Dar on the way to Aqra. It was by a river – and simply lovely. Unfortunately neither Isabel nor I had swimming things and so just paddled and sat about. It was very hot and we got nicely sunburnt – and also ate an enormous picnic lunch...

The Sinclairs had asked the entire British community (8 or 10!) in for drinks at 6.30...It was so nice as we met everyone. There were the Ross-Thomases who are British Council, the Smiths who are Stephen Lynch and Co., Tony and Robin, the Evans' (he is the forestry expert up at Salahuddin – and there they are the *only* Britishers) a delightful couple, and Peter Jordan of the Ottoman Bank...They were all so nice to us, asking how long we were staying etc. and what we were going to do on Monday etc. etc. In the end we had quite a full day on Monday – and highly social!...

(Oh! I've forgotten all about Jonah and the whale after all that!! When we started off on Sunday morning with Tony in the car, he took us first to Nebi Yunis (Tomb of Jonah) which is a little village and mosque on one of the mounds of old Nineveh. The mosque is supposed to contain Jonah's tomb and we were allowed in. It is the first time I'd been inside a mosque, and we had to take off our shoes and leave them outside! Then we walked in – and it just seems to be a series of carpeted rooms and passages, with odd mosaics and passages from the Quran dotted about. Jonah's tomb was *enormous* and Isabel and I were sure it contained the whale as well!! Also hanging on the wall were two huge teeth which the Mullah assured us had belonged to Jonah – but I thought not! Anyway it was interesting!).

We had been asked to tea with Peter Jordan...Having discovered Isabel was definitely going to Istanbul in June, and that I was still wavering, he said, 'Why not come in September when I will be there, and stay with us on the island, as it will save you money and be a good base for Istanbul?!' Isn't it kind of him? And it is an absolute answer to a maiden's prayer, as I was almost giving up the idea of going at all, as it would be so expensive etc. and not knowing anyone to show one around. Now of course it will be wonderful, as his grandmother, mother and at least *six* elderly maiden aunts all live on the island which is about 12 miles from Istanbul in the Sea of Marmora! So it will all be quite proper and everything – and as he says, I will be well chaperoned. He has a young brother at Sandhurst but he will have gone back by September, so that really he would be quite glad of someone young to go around with – and it will be marvellous for me! He was awfully funny about it and said I must write and get your permission. So will you write quickly saying, 'Yes' and then I can let him know my decision and he will then write and warn Mama, Grandmama and six maiden aunties!!!!'…

Baghdad   *21 May 1951*

'…Peter Jordan paid Baghdad a surprise visit on Saturday on business…Peter asked if I'd written to you yet. I said I had and he was terribly pleased and will write to his mother as soon as I hear from you that it is alright! I thought that he might have regretted his hasty decision by now but, on the contrary, he seemed very thrilled that I wanted to come. It is the sort of holiday that is going to suit me down to the ground as he said he wanted me to understand that he wanted a cheap holiday and hoped I'd be happy swimming etc., and pottering around with boats!! Could anything be more lovely – as the very last thing I would want to do is to dash around night clubs etc! I am quite glad I'm not going till September, as then the heat will be over when I come back and I will be nicely refreshed after the summer and alright until I get home! He is a funny chap, and apparently only about 27 or 28. He looks much more and has got very stout, but I was pleased to note he has now shaved off his moustache since last week! He is a Roman Catholic – and an ardent one at that – so that is a good thing, as it will be quite a solid bulwark if you see what I mean!! I am just slightly dubious of what Ralph is going to think about it all – as people always get funny ideas don't they?…

Oh! *another* engagement for Baghdad! Archie Rendall (strike off the list!!) is engaged to Sheila Davis. Isn't it exciting, and very suitable I feel. Sheila is divorced actually but such a nice sensible person and awfully suited to Archie's rather stolid Scots temperament'…

Baghdad   *1 June 1951*

'…My dear, you'll never guess what happened on Wednesday evening! I had been to choir practice, and then for a drink at the Club with Derek and co…At about 10.30 I was just going to get into bed – all in my nightdress, hair net etc., when the phone went! I answered it and a man's voice asked if that was Air Lodge?; I explained that it was the Staff House and the voice then asked if I was Miss Borlase. I said, 'yes' – and the voice then said, 'Well, this is Dave Morgan here!!!' He was on his way through in the Attacker, flying it out to Karachi…He asked if we'd like to go to Abdullah's, and after saying, 'no', firmly, both Isabel and I decided that that was rather inhospitable, so we said, 'yes'! So I dashed off and dressed again, and mercifully woke up with a bang! He came round and we had a quick drink and then the three of us set off for Abdullah's. It was grand seeing him again, and I am glad we made the effort as with those characters I always feel they are living terribly intensely – every moment must be used – just in case they are killed tomorrow. He came round to the office next morning just before going off and collected his bathing things from the bottom of the filing cabinet, where they have reposed since last August! He isn't coming back via Baghdad, but is going to give two of his friends our phone number who are coming through at the end of June! We tried to extract their names – but all we managed to find out is that one goes by the name of 'Chunky' Horne, and the other – 'Peewee' Judd!! Have you ever heard anything like it?! Dave was in grand form – and I've got a standing invitation to visit him and his wife and family when I go home, as they live at King's Sombourne (?) near Stockbridge, or somewhere. Rather fun!! It quite cheered Isabel and I on our way…

We had a terrific (in length only) day at Habbaniya on Sunday, and although basically it was grand fun, it all went on too long and the company was too ghastly for words. Johnny Locklack (who is a nice kindly chap) collected Pat and I and we had a jolly good run down and reached the Lake and Boat Club at about 10.00 a.m. There we joined up with various Embassy and O.R. clerks etc., which wasn't too good as they were a noisy hearty lot. However, it was just Pat's idea of heaven (Butlins Holiday Camp!), so I had to grin, and shriek with laughter at their jokes etc. (Oh! dear! Don't I sound snobby and stuck up, but you do understand what I mean don't you?!). It was a perfect day anyway and the lake was heaven. We had a wonderful swim and then went sailing. I went out with some R.A.F. type by myself and had a simply grand time as he was a monosyllabic character, and let me sail it all by myself. So I was perfectly happy – the first sail since Cyprus last year! The others went in another sailing boat – and there must have been about 10 of them all shrieking and pushing each other overboard etc., so we left them to it! We had a very late lunch at the Boat Club, but it was jolly good when we got it. Then we all swam again and lazed about. Then Johnny Locklack suddenly announced that there was some sort of 'hop' on in

the camp at the Royal Order of the Buffaloes Club (apparently
the Poor Man's Freemasonry Society!). Anyway, I expressed a
desire to get back to Baghdad about 8.00 or 9.00 p.m. but this
was *so* unpopular that I had to abandon all hope. So we stayed
and stayed and it would have been quite nice if we hadn't had
an appalling man called Breakspeare tagging on all the time. He
works in the Despatch Room at the Embassy and is everyone's
bugbear! He isn't too bad, but is so exhausting! We had a lovely
supper of eggs and chips etc. down at the Boat Club, which
really was rather lovely. Then I was perfectly ready to go home
– but not so Johnny, Breakspeare and Pat. So we went back to
the R.A.F. Camp and eventually found the 'Buffs'. It was a
ghastly dingy room, with about a dozen or so of the absolute
dregs of the R.A.F. BORs [British Other Ranks] lounging
about. Anyway we stayed and chatted to them for a bit and had
the odd dance. It wasn't too bad and certainly brightened up
their Sunday evening, so I didn't mind that. Then we drove
back and must have got in about 11.30 or so. So it wasn't really
too bad but I don't think I have ever been so tired!…

Baghdad   *4 June 1951*

'…(Oh! I nearly forgot to tell you, Pat rang me up on
Saturday morning to tell me that Ralph had got back on Friday
evening – via Basra – as she had seen him at a cocktail party –
so I had been *hoping* he would ring me). Anyway I sped down
to the phone and it was Neville. He wanted to know if Isabel
and I would like to have dinner with Ralph and him on
Wednesday night, so I explained about her being on leave, and
so Elizabeth is coming instead! Having said all this, he then
said, 'By the way, we've got Ralph back with us' – so I said,
'Really' – in very surprised tones – all quite absurd!! Then he
said, 'I think Ralph would like a word with you' – and then
there were all sorts of remarks passed, of which I only caught

one or two. But eventually Ralph came to the phone and said, 'Hullo, Mary.' GORGEOUS!! He said…'I must come over to the Railway Club on Tuesday afternoon (today!) and swim'. Anyway he said he'd ring me about it last night – but as usual hasn't!! I am getting quite used to his vague ways now – and luckily I went out to dinner and didn't stay listening for the phone…

…Well, here I am again in one of my famous predicaments! What shall I do if Ralph hasn't rung by lunchtime?! Do I do nothing, or do I ring and remind him, or what?!! I think men are the end! Judging by previous times – he'll just turn up. But unless I ring and find out *when* – he will probably catch me in my office dress, with face greasy and shining – awful thought!!! I will add to this if I've time before the mail goes tomorrow morning…

Wednesday. Men *are* the end!! It is just as well I didn't finish this off last night as I was in such a bad temper. Ralph never rang up – and I think he must have forgotten. Anyway, I hung around for ages and eventually rang the Mess – to find that he had gone out! So I went off and had a swim at the Club – in a vile temper with everyone. I came home and pottered about, composing wonderful angry outbursts for Ralph – but when he rang at 7.15 I couldn't get a word in edgeways!! He said he was *frightfully* sorry (but offered no explanation!) and said I must come today'…

Baghdad   *14 June 1951*

'…We dashed down to the Railway Club last Friday evening for farewell drinks with Neville…Next morning I was up with the lark and had an *awful* job waking Pat – as we were going down to see Neville off. However, we got down there in very good time – and the Walters were there too, and Ralph came along later!! We went right inside the Viking and inspected it, and Ralph took a *lovely* photograph of Neville standing on top of the steps. It was *very* sad indeed – as he is such a nice person and looked *very* nice on Sunday morning...

Oh! Ralph rang up *again* on Wednesday evening (all most encouraging?!!!) to tell me the latest bulletin on the car, and apparently Tom Walters got it going at last and now it is alright...I am dying to see it. All most exciting!...

June is fairly whizzing along compared with May! However, don't take things seriously Mummy – as I think you are you know!! I'm not yet. I'm dying my level best to interest myself in others for the good of my soul – but scope is limited!! However, not to worry – what's MEANT to be will be. Nighty night'!!

Baghdad   *20 June 1951*

'...Anyway, I've heard from Peter Jordan at last – such a nice letter – and aging Grandmother says of course I can come, as long as I don't mind just pottering about the island, swimming etc. So isn't that *grand*?! I was getting rather dubious about the whole thing and nearly decided to scrub it – go to Cyprus and ask you to join me there...

On Sunday morning...O course I was just dressing when the doorbell went – and it was Ralph!! I had to dash down – hairbrush in hand – and look at the CAR!! It's the most gorgeous thing you've ever seen!! It is a little two-seater M.G. (brand new) – red – bright and polished! I shrieked my delight – and I really must have been jolly enthusiastic over it because he even showed me the engine (which conveyed nothing!!), but I thought that showed he felt I was interested. It's got two carburettors – I can remember that much!!? Anyway, I had the most *gorgeous* day...We had lunch at the Club, lovely curry too! Then he asked if I'd like to see his boat, so we went off in the car along the River Bund to see the boat. It is practically finished and looks terribly nice…Being an open car – the sun beats down like nobody's business – but it was cool going along by the river…He *must* be nice you know as he said that he has three sisters – and two of them are called Mary and Elizabeth! The third is Hilary, and he has a younger brother…

Last night was one of the best evenings I've spent in Baghdad – or rather out of it! Derek J. asked me on a *masquf party down the river – and it was a full moon, warm, and perfectly lovely and so different from last time when we were a great noisy, drunken mob! This time there were only 11 of us.

…We went down in quite a small open launch, and beer was the only drink. (*Much* more sensible!!). The trip down was simply lovely – and it really was beautiful. The moon was enormous – and made a pathway over the water to the boat. We arrived on Pig Island eventually and the boys cooked the masquf. I had to smoke to keep away the insects, but otherwise it was perfect. The fish was served up on the gangplank!! We just plunged into it with our fingers and it *was* delicious!! They had asked me to bring my gramophone (against my principles!!) but I did and we had some music. They had rather sensibly got the cars to come down the river as far as the island – so that we didn't have to go all the way back by boat – which would have made it so late. As it was, we left Pig Island at 12.30, and I was home by 1.30…

Baghdad   *23 June 1951*

'…Ralph…is coming along in his car tonight to collect me. Isn't that fun?!!! LIFE IS MARVELLOUS – isn't it?!! I have got a sore throat, and E[lizabeth] has an awful cold – and it is far too hot. It was 108 degrees the day before yesterday – and ten times hotter yesterday. My office is *honestly* an oven – but AIN'T LIFE FUN!!!

*Masquf – a large fish known as the Tigris salmon split open and roasted on charcoal.

Hope you are all well and not as hot as I am. Must fly now. Tons and tons of love. Mary.

P.S. I think the heat's affecting my brain'!!!! ?!!!

★   ★   ★

The Shrove Tuesday Dance at the Alwiyah Club.

Sunday morning, Alwiyah Club Pool.

Picnic in date grove with the Rays.

Arch of Ctesiphon.

Sunday at Habbaniya.

Officers' Club, Habbaniya.

British Vice-Consulate, Mosul.

CHAPTER 8

Baghdad
10.07.51 - 27.10.51

'I have had the most lovely holiday, and feel *much* better now…

I had an extremely comfortable journey up…We got into Mosul at 7.00 a.m. and Peter was there to meet me…Peter had to work on Wednesday morning, so I spent a lazy morning…I didn't go round the town or anything as it was so hot…We set off about 5.30 p.m. It is a 3-hour drive altogether, but quite interesting. At Erbil…we stopped to fix up my return journey. Erbil is the town which has been built on the same spot for centuries and centuries – in fact it is *the* oldest in the world. When you approach it across the plain it looks like a medieval castle, as the old town is built on top of a round hill. The new town is below and round the bottom.

'…The drive from Erbil up to Salahuddin was lovely – as it was all hairpin bends etc! We arrived at the Evans' bungalow at about 9.00, just in time for supper. They *are* a nice couple and so simple and natural…I slept in the spare room and Peter was on a camp bed in the hall. I slept like a log and wouldn't have woken if Peter hadn't roused me at some ungodly hour (6.00 a.m.) to go swimming. Actually it was *heavenly* at that hour, and we swam before breakfast every morning! We had the most delicious late breakfasts of melon, cornflakes, eggs and coffee. I ate like a horse all the time I was up there!! In the mornings we sat about, read, and I usually went for a walk with a book and camera as it was so heavenly outside. I would walk for some

time and then find a tree and read my book. It was never too
hot even at about mid-day for that, and there was a lovely cool
breeze. The first afternoon we all went to see the Rowanduz
Gorge!! I am so thrilled I've seen it before I leave, as it really is
magnificent. It is 3 hours north of Salahuddin, and a lovely run
through mountains, plains, and Kurdish villages etc. to get
there. We went right through the Gorge and back and I took
heaps of photos which I *hope* will come out. It is a tremendous
height on either side, and there is a terribly strong stream
rushing down it – lots of waterfalls – and overhanging rocks
etc. It was the old caravan route to Persia, and we actually met
an old Kurd who is chief of a tribe up there, and Jack told us
that he had killed about 50 people as he used to be one of the
chief brigands who robbed the caravans!! Ever so exciting!!!…

The next day…we finished in great style with a proper
Kurdish ★'Cusi' at lunch time. We had it in a hut made of
leaves (known as 'Kapris') and very cool. The Kurd on my right
kept pulling out lumps of solid FAT and plonking them on my
plate! Apparently fat is regarded as the best part!! I swallowed
one bit with quantities of rice, but couldn't face any more –
ugh!! However, it didn't matter and as one felt full (Zur Pirar
in Kurdish!!) you just left the table and had your hands washed.
I just nipped up in time when I saw a hand delving for more
dainty morsels of fat. Anyway, I took photos of the remains of
the Cusi – and several of the Kurds in their national dress
seething with daggers and revolvers etc. etc.! Unfortunately we
had to dash away as I had to leave at 3.30 as the train from Erbil
left at 5.15…

Now for the awful thing – I can't *stand* Peter Jordan! He's
simply ghastly – and says horrible crude things all day long. I
don't think they're a bit funny, and really rather revolting.
Anyway, I made it *perfectly* clear that I wasn't in the least bit
attracted to him (without being rude of course!) and I think he

★Cusi – lamb roasted whole, with rice.

realises that now and won't be difficult or anything. Isabel now admits that his mother asked her just how fond I was of 'her Peter' etc. etc. – obviously making a big romance of it. So Isabel – dear Isabel – gave her to understand that I had just millions of men friends – and I was out every night etc. etc. – all totally untrue!! However, I gather she gave her to understand that I wasn't at all chasing 'her Peter'. So I think it's alright to go now – and perfectly safe and everything. The thing is that I shall try to contact some of the people Isabel met, so that I can get away from Jordan family undiluted. I desperately want to go to Istanbul now and it does sound such a lovely place. Also, I think Peter realises (from experience in Salahuddin) that I shall want to shoot off by myself. So that's alright isn't it? It is a pity I don't like him as it would have been *much* more fun with someone nice. So it is really a *very* good thing I got to know Peter so well in Salahuddin, as now I think he understands I'm not interested in *him* personally'…

Baghdad   *Friday 13 July 1951*

'…I am so thrilled about your heatwave, but please don't expect me to sympathise with you as the temperature has just shot up out here. Yesterday the official temperature was 115 degrees!! Also, at the coolest point of the night it only went down to 85 degrees!! Today when we left the office the temperature was 119$\frac{1}{2}$ degrees!!! The official temperature is usually about one degree less, but all the same 118 degrees is hotter than I've ever had it yet. Last year the highest recorded was 116 degrees for one day in late August (when I was away), and it is only mid-July now – with six hot weeks ahead! Isn't it fun – I wonder if we shall reach the 120 degree mark. Anyway, I am still alive and well, drinking like a fish, and dripping over everything…

I hardly had any time in the office today, as I had to come

back with a Czech R.A.F. Officer and check (!!) inventories. It was a gruelling, hot job, counting forks, knives, etc. but we drank quantities of squash etc. and in the end it wasn't worth my going back to the office!…

P.S. Phew – poof – drip – splash'!

Baghdad   *17 July 1951*

'…My dear, Baghdad (or rather the people) has suddenly got terribly nice again!! I don't know whether you gathered it from my letters or not, but in May we *all* got depressed. All my friends seemed to have left, and Derek had got engaged etc…But now, after my little leave – I have quite recovered. Mainly because we have met some awfully nice people recently…Adrian Mansvelt, the 2nd Secretary at the Dutch Legation – is a very nice person. Then there is a nice I.P.C. boy called Tom Hallawell, who is P.A. to one of the big cheeses of the I.P.C. The nicest of all, whom I only met on Friday, is Col. Mostert's (Technical Adviser, Iraqi Airways) successor!! It is very amusing, as we *all* expected some elderly gentleman to come in his place – as Col. M. was nearly 60!! Instead we have an exceptionally handsome young man of 36 – no wife!!…His name is Donald Bennett, and he comes from Nottingham. I found out his age, but none of us can find out if he ever had a wife! He says no, to the ordinary questioner apparently, but someone has started up a rumour that he is divorced or something. However we don't know! He was *very* helpful over my crawl, and has been the most assistance so far. I can actually *do* the crawl now, although it doesn't look very professional, but it is better than it was…

My dear – do you remember me saying I'd checked inventories with a Czech officer?!! Well – I must have touched the cockles of his heart or something as I had the most *amazing* letter from him, written from Habb. on Sunday!!! My picture was still with him etc. etc. and he had been captivated by my voice calling 'Abdullah' – were my beautiful eyes always so strict etc. etc.!!!! Honestly, I was flabbergasted – and I've never had a letter like that in my life. I asked Isabel's advice – and she says do nothing, which is easy enough – but oh! dear – what awful predicaments I do seem to get into! Anyway I shall keep it as a souvenir and show my grandchildren!! Have I really *strict* eyes'?!!!…

Baghdad   *20 July 1951*

'I can't wait for Sunday – (a) because Ralph should come back, and (b) it is letter day now. I have quite recovered from my infatuation for Mr Bennett – and so has Isabel, I think!…

Of course I think the R.A.F. are mad. The queerest little Flying Officer came in yesterday – and proceeded to wobble all the furniture – to see if it needed repairing. He then said he had a message for me from the Czech. My heart sank and Isabel was no help as she only giggled! I said something about inventories etc, but he was too mysterious for words, and with much raising of the eyebrows he said he thought there was more to it than that!! The Czech wants me to go to an entirely Czech dinner party in Baghdad – but I go out every *single* night!! Even Isabel says the queerest things go on at Czech dinners, so I'm not going'!!!…

Baghdad   *24 July 1951*

'How wonderful, gorgeous and marvellous about Ralph coming [to see you at Wilton]!!…I honestly thought that when it came to the point, he wouldn't do more than just ring up. But how *terribly* good of him to motor bike all that way. I am so glad you like him – I knew you would! Isn't he nice? Haven't I got good taste?! Anyway, thank you very much for letting me know so quickly, and I am just longing for your next letter to hear all the detailed impressions. You must tell me *everything* that was said – and you didn't say anything AWFUL did you, Mum?!! Oh! dear! I am so excited about it… I am longing to see him now and hear all about you both – just how you are looking etc. etc. We shall have plenty to talk about anyway!…

Thank you for considering my underwear question – as always a very last consideration with me! My pyjamas are alright for the winter – not beautiful – but adequate! Then the three nighties I've got will do for the summer. I have got plenty of winter vests, but only those threadbare ones of yours for the summer. What I shall need is decent petticoats and pants etc. – of a rather more dainty nature than previously. However, I really think it is very difficult for you to get them as you won't know exactly what I want. I will send you my measurements later…

My dear, I thought I would have to spend the weekend in an Iraqi gaol, but all was well. I had forgotten to renew my residence permit in time and they nearly took me to court, but our interpreter went down and talked nicely to them and said I was so frightened of going to prison etc., that they relented. I am still trying to extricate my passport and residence permit though – I feel like a displaced person at the moment without either…

After church Isabel, Pat, Derek and I all went to dinner with Don as he had the Station Manager (Iraqi Airways) up from Basra…We had a lovely dinner – cold buffet – on the lawn and then he put on his wire-recorder and then it played back to us all the things we'd said. I have *never* in my life heard anything so appalling as my voice recorded (unless it is my voice in real life!). This awful affected high squeak kept coming out – actually it was absolutely killing and I nearly split myself with laughing. Isabel found she had the most appalling Oxford accent, and Pat was broad Cockney. Only the men seemed to sound fairly normal'!…

Baghdad   *31 July 1951*

'I was just dressing at 7.00 a.m. on Saturday when the phone went – then Isabel dashed upstairs to tell me it was Ralph!!…He asked if I could come over swimming at the Railway club on Sunday morning…

On Sunday morning I was all ready – wearing the pretty blue check you sent me – when he arrived. He came in and had some iced coffee and we all talked as Isabel and Elizabeth were there. Then we went off in the red M.G. over to the Railway Club and he started telling me *all* about it. He was wonderful – as throughout the day he kept remembering little bits of this and that and things you'd said etc. Anyway, I think you've 'passed A.1' – as he was fully of praise for everything. He said Wilton was the most beautiful old town – and he simply loved the garden and the house and said we really had the most beautiful furniture and pictures etc. Honestly, he really *did* love it all, I'm sure, and said it did him good. Daddy, he thinks you are *terribly* nice, and he told me how well you'd got on and talked and talked about everything from Gladstone to trout in Tehran. Mummy, he thought you were terribly nice too, and judging by the amount you all talked, I can't *think* how it all fitted into $2^{1}/_{2}$ hours!!…

I had a simply *lovely* day with Ralph – just perfect!…We had a lovely lunch – and then of course the phone went for Ralph from the Airport, and they wanted him to test the Dove – which had something wrong with it. So he suddenly said, 'Would I like to come up too'!! So I spent a portion of Sunday afternoon flying over Baghdad!! It all seemed too easy for words, and he just had to give my name in to the Traffic Manager (so as next-of-kin could be informed – according to

Nobby!!). We went down to the airport immediately after
lunch, and of course it was boiling inside the Dove as it had
been standing in the sun. Ralph piloted it, and there was just an
engineer up in the front, and me. I had to sit in the back until
we were airborne, and then Ralph beckoned me forward and I
stood just behind him while he pointed out everything. It was
absolutely thrilling – and most interesting seeing Baghdad from
the air! It looks much pleasanter I must say, as one can see
masses of date groves etc. The river twists and twists, and of
course I always thought it was pretty straight. It just shows! We
flew all round and *just* saw our house, and a tiny blue patch
which was the Alwiyah Club pool!! We picked out everything,
and I had a particularly good view of the mosques and golden
domes of Kadhimain. Of course I began to feel sick as it was
terribly hot, and we were all just *pouring* sweat. Luckily we only
stayed up about 25 minutes, and so I didn't have time to be
really ill!!…

We got back to the Mess and cooled down and Ralph made
some tea – and we talked. During the course of the day I had
poured out all my various little excitements – such as Czechs
etc. – and I also told him about Istanbul, Jordan family etc. etc.
Oh! When he asked about Salahuddin he said rather pointedly
that he gathered I'd enjoyed the scenery, so had you said
anything?!! A propos of all this he suddenly came out with an
amazing story about himself. He'd had a letter waiting for him
in the Mess when we got in at lunchtime, which he'd rather
gawped over! Anyway he proceeded to tell me (in strict
confidence!) that the wife of the couple who have the flat at the
top of their house (just like ours!) in Epsom was making a pass
at him. Apparently last time he was at home when his mother
was away, he and his young brother fed upstairs with this
couple, as there was no-one else in the house. Ralph said he
never noticed anything until one day she had clutched his hand
at a fair, and he'd got the shock of his life when he'd realised!

He also found the husband none too friendly – what a set-up. Then this time he hoped it would be alright as his mother would be at home, but of course she was being ill up in Lincoln! Then the last night before he came back here, her husband was out and she poured out all her woes to Ralph – and indeed it is a pathetic story as her husband is R.C. etc. etc. And then Ralph had a letter from her this Sunday!! He was awfully sweet about it actually, and said that of course it was probably because she was getting bored with Epsom – and then someone fresh came from the East – with fresh ideas etc. Anyway, he poured it all out to me and said, wasn't life complicated. Wasn't it nice of him though?…

It really was a perfect day and we got on so well'…

Baghdad   *7 August 1951*

'…But, Mummy, you *mustn't* tell people about Ralph, *please*. I should hate to think anyone knew about my private affairs out here. Have you told Maria Clapp, because Michael hasn't written to me for *months*. Please, please don't tell anyone in future about me, as I shall have to stop telling you *ALL*, and I couldn't bear that. I should hate to think of people gossiping and saying that of course I only went abroad to 'catch' someone, and then everyone speculating as to whether I shall get engaged or not, when of course I shan't. If Ralph ever *were* to do anything, which I very much doubt, it wouldn't be until after I got home anyway…

Oh! I rang Peter Jordan yesterday evening, as I heard via Nigel awful rumours of 'Grandma' being very ill, so I concluded that it was all off. Anyway, I started off on those lines but Peter wasn't a bit helpful and I'm really no further on than I was before. He said that the position is that his Grandma's hip has come unset again and that she is laid up on the island, being nursed by Mother – who hasn't been too well – and in addition there is the chance that Grandma may pop off any day now. With this doleful picture in front of me, there seemed no possible hope that they could want me, so I said quite definitely that I wouldn't come. Peter was quite hopeless and said that it was entirely up to *me*, as he thought they were quite willing to have me. He says the house is big and they have servants etc. and that it won't make any difference, but I still think it would be rather rude to go don't you? Anyway, I said all this and he rather took it that I didn't want to go, because I might have a dull time with them all ill. So he insists on cabling Mama and asking so that I shall know definitely one way or the other. However if she says yes, I can still come, I am sure I oughtn't to, do you? I think Peter hopes I will come so that he will have an excuse not to play attendance on Grandma all day long, as he will have to 'entertain the guest'. So here I am, no further on, but if they can't have me I don't fancy staying in a city like Istanbul all on my own, as even Isabel says it is the sort of place where men follow one about!!...'

Baghdad   *10 August 1951*

'I just happened to call in at the Club on Wednesday afternoon on my way home from the Doctor's, and there was Ralph playing water polo. I apologised for the dinner and of course he said that he honestly hadn't noticed anything wrong – so that was alright. He said he was sorry he had been so tired, but they'd had quite a bit of trouble which he proceeded to relate. He'd flown to Cairo on Tuesday as you know, and actually it was the Iraqi pilot who was flying and Ralph was just co-pilot. Anyway when they were taking off from Damascus on the way home the pilot did a swerve on the runway and then did what is known as 'over-correcting'. It all sounds very technical and complicated, but anyway I gather it was a nasty moment and Ralph had to knock his hands off the controls, open up his engine, and take over. By a miracle he got it out of the swing, but by this time they were off the end of the runway and he had to take off off a ploughed field! He then found that the rear wheel wouldn't go up, but had no possible means of knowing what was the matter with it. So of course when they reached Baghdad it was rather an unpleasant landing as the wheel collapsed at once and they bumped all over the place. So he said that honestly he was so glad to reach the ground again he hadn't noticed the dinner. Of course the trouble is that the authorities are awful about these things – and the unfair part is that it is always the captain of the plane's responsibility – no matter what happens. So I gather he was rather worried about results. All this was a strict confidence of course as they are not allowed to talk about accidents – in relation to the pilots as people lose their confidence in the particular Iraqi gentleman concerned!…

As for Dinah's wonderful and most generous offer – I just can't thank her enough! Does she really mean it – because I shall definitely come to Athens – I haven't heard the result of Peter's cable yet, but in any case I can't believe it would be polite to go now'…

Baghdad   *17 August 1951*

'I had a simply GORGEOUS evening last night – I was having dinner etc. with Ralph if you remember. Elizabeth and Isabel were having a dinner party, so I had a drink with them until Ralph arrived. Having been with them for about two minutes I suddenly got up and said goodbye – so they must have thought I was mad!! Ralph collected me in the car and then we went to the Alwiyah Club and sat on the lawn and had a drink. We had a very good dinner and then saw the film which was called 'Dancing in the Dark' – an American musical and quite enjoyable – at least it wasn't anything sordid or depressing. I was afraid that Ralph would want to go immediately after the film, but he didn't and suggested that we should stay and have a drink. So we stayed and actually *danced*!! I hadn't ever danced with him except at that Mess party last December – so it was great fun. He isn't a bad dancer, but rather hesitant. It was jolly funny as he is the sort of person who says, 'look out' just before they do a step so that one is warned!! Anyway we didn't get on at all badly – and it sure will set the tongues wagging! We didn't stay till the end of the dancing, but left about 12.30 and drove back along the river bank. It looked simply lovely as it is full moon tonight and it was beautifully cool…

Of course what I was dreading happened yesterday! Peter Jordan got through to me in the office, and said that he'd had a cable back signed by his grandmother saying, 'Expecting Mary'. So it was just too dreadful for words, and I had to say that honestly I had already decided I would be in the way etc. etc. and made other plans. All very embarrassing and difficult – but I am so glad really that it is all over and definite that I can't go. At any rate Isabel and I know that Mrs Jordan really will be pleased I can't go – as she wanted 'her Peter' all to herself anyway. Isabel says I have done the right thing as she is quite sure I wouldn't have enjoyed that household. Apparently Mama suddenly goes down on her knees to the Virgin Mary at unexpected moments – well really – what a holiday! So now for Greece!…

P.S. I happened to walk past Mr Gillibrand at the pool yesterday afternoon – he immediately started singing 'at the wedding of Mary Borlase' – so I suppose he'd seen us on Thursday night!!

Baghdad   *21 August 1951*

'I honestly do need my leave now, as I just can't work up

enthusiasm for anything, (except Ralph!!!), I get terribly sleepy and lethargic, bad-tempered and goodness knows what else. Worst of all when I'm alone I keep repeating things over and over again in my head, like 'I must do my washing and ironing, washing and ironing, washing and ironing etc. etc.' I am indeed in a bad way!! I just can't even think about my 21st birthday at the moment, and don't even want a party out here – because of the effort and expense – but of course I do really and when I get back I shall get around to it!!'

Baghdad   *24 August 1951*

'We saw quite an amusing musical film last night with the Padre, but when he came to start the car again after, he couldn't fit the key in the lock as someone had tried to force it!! Wasn't it dreadful? Of course he had rather stupidly left one door open, but had told a policeman to keep an eye on it. We stood around for hours until a crowd of willing Arabs all tried to set the entire car on fire by peering at its innards with lighted matches! In the end we had to leave it and so the Venerable Archdeacon of Iraq and Saudi Arabia was to be seen travelling home in an Arabana with two ladies!! We had an excellent dinner – being rather famished by this time – and then the Padre had to take us home in a taxi. Poor Padre – awful things always seem to be happening to his car'.

Baghdad   *28 August 1951*

'I think Ralph really *is* awfully shy you know – he was terribly sweet last night, but he is obviously a bit nervous or something because if he puts a hand on my shoulder or anything – he removes it hastily!! Still – isn't it *nice* – a thousand times more so than the Perry Fellowes of this world – ugh!!!'…

Baghdad   *7 September 1951*

'Last night was terrific fun…It was a *terribly* nice party and
Ralph quite obviously enjoyed it immensely…Ralph and I left
at 11.30 p.m. as he is flying today, and according to Isabel we
didn't miss a thing as after we'd gone it got rather dull. Ralph
drove me all the way home – *AND* – he held my *hand tight all
the way* practically. *Very* encouraging – and he *was* so nice'!!!!…

Baghdad   *11 September 1951*

'My darling Mummy,
This letter is really intended for you both, but as it will no
doubt contain a few feminine sentimentalities, I thought it had
better be addressed to you! Please don't think I am stealing
office notepaper, (which I am) but it is two old sheets which I
can't use for typing official letters – so rather than see it rot in
the drawer…
Well – the day of days has dawned at last and I'm off this
evening [on leave to Athens]…
…Ralph asked me if I could come to dinner and the cinema
again *last* night! Of course I'd meant to be packing, hairwashing, and goodness knows what, but I said 'yes'. And
luckily, I'd got everything so well organised that it was no effort
at all!!! Anyway as Ralph was flying yesterday he brought me
home fairly early, and came in for a drink and to collect his
book. (It was *very* nice, – we were standing looking at the book
and he put his arm round me – and then kissed me!!). Do you
mind me telling you all this – because you are the only *possible*
person I could tell – and you don't think I'm sentimental and
sloppy do you?!! He stroked my hair and said something about
'hair so often blown by the wind' – from his car! Anyway, then
he went off – and it was only about 10.30 – but for some
unknown reason I wasn't in bed till quarter to twelve as I was

floating around in a dream!! Of course yesterday in the office I couldn't even subtract two from three and kept making the answer nine!!! (I've got it bad!!).

Oh! I must tell you – the Padre apparently once told Paul that I was the most level-headed person of my age he'd ever met!! Isn't that amazing – and even Isabel said she quite agreed. I don't know if that's a compliment or not – but I thought it would please you!!!'…

Mary used her 1951 allowance of local leave to visit Greece. She travelled by Nairn bus to Beirut and thence flew to Athens, where she stayed with some friends of her parents.

Baghdad   *4 October 1951*

'Just a very hurried scribble to let you know I'm safe back in Baghdad. For once I don't mind a bit returning, and am thoroughly looking forward to the next six months…

…I've just attempted to ring Ralph – FLYING of course! I gather the pilgrims are now returning again – they would be – however, plenty of time ahead!

There is a handicap tennis tournament coming off soon which Isabel has put us down for in the Ladies Doubles. I have entered for Singles and just *pray* that Ralph will ask me for Mixed Doubles, but apparently he hasn't been seen at the club for about a fortnight – so won't even have seen the notice'…

Baghdad   *12 October 1951*

'We are playing tennis hectically now…Then the Handicap Tournament starts next week. I am playing with John Marshall in the Mixed Doubles and we shouldn't do too badly. The others (Isabel and Elizabeth) made me wait for ages until Ralph asked me – but of course I had to let John know in reasonable time. Anyway, I would have looked a fool if I'd said no, as yesterday I see a 'Miss Stevens and A.B.R. Watts' are playing together. Terrific conjectures as to who on earth this Miss Stevens is, as none of us have ever heard of her! Ralph hasn't entered for anything else though...

'Better to have loved and lost...' I suppose. Well – anyway I must tell you the sad tale. You know I couldn't get through to the Mess last weekend. Then on Monday night he was on a late flying service. I tried again on Tuesday night and he'd just gone out, but they said they'd give him a message to ring me. By this time I was beginning to lose hope, and then on Wednesday when I was at choir practice he rang at last! Then he rang again at 10.15 p.m. but of course I was out again. Elizabeth spoke to him both times and said he sounded *most* anxious to speak to me, so I was *quite* cheered up, especially as he said he'd been on the Jeddah run etc. and very busy all the time. However by the time I got in yesterday after tennis I was all depressed again – and so rang up there and then. I got him at last...He was terribly brief on the phone – and kept saying, 'Don't tell me a thing'. So anyway he asked if I was booked up tonight – and so I'm having dinner with him this evening'...

Saturday morning. Oh! Great relief. Everything's perfectly *ALRIGHT*! Can you believe it – and all that worry and commotion about nothing. 'Miss Stevens' is the daughter of a man over the other side who asked Ralph to coach her at tennis. He even admitted that he 'had been dragged into the tournament' – so that's alright...He brought me home about 10.45 p.m. – and it was gorgeous to be in the red M.G. again – I'd thought I'd seen the last of it!! He was terribly apologetic about not getting hold of me before – and said I'd been out when he rang too. And everything's gorgeous – and the world has taken on a more colourful hue this morning (though it's pouring with rain!!)'.

Baghdad   *16 October 1951*

'…The dance was excellent at the Railway Club and I thoroughly enjoyed it…I ate an *enormous* buffet supper – and made the mistake of saying to Robert that I wasn't really hungry to start with. 'My God, what on earth are you like when you *are* hungry' was his comment'!!! I noted a *very* pretty girl (about 16 or 17) in pale mauve net – and mentally decided 'Miss Stevens' – and it is!!! However, I don't think (touch wood hard) I need worry yet!! Too young for Ralph anyway'!…

Baghdad   *19 October 1951*

'The weather is simply perfect now! It has gone very cold at nights, but beautifully sunny in the day. I am still sleeping on the roof, and I am going to have a third blanket as I don't think two will be quite enough soon. It is a gorgeous feeling when you wake up and poke your nose out into the cold!!…

It was rather a large and unwieldy and slightly ill-assorted dinner party at Jack's…However it wasn't too bad and at dinner I was between Ralph and Dick, which was nice. Ralph was *so* nice – and even when he was talking at the far end of the room he was always looking over to see how I was getting along etc…At about 12.10 he looked up and caught my eye – and we decided to leave. I was *so* glad as I was dropping by that time, and apparently the others didn't get away until after 2 a.m.! We went home, and he came in for a second (15 minutes or so) to collect the Byron – and was *very* nice'!!!!!…

Of course Ralph couldn't play tennis or come to dinner and cinema with us yesterday because of [flying to] Beirut – but we had a very pleasant evening. In the end we just had John Goodge and Hugh Seymour – the two nice boys from Abadan. Hugh comes from Westbury and his father is Sir…Seymour and has been Ambassador here, there and everywhere'…

Baghdad   *23 October 1951*

'Only another fortnight now before the Great Day [21st birthday]. I am getting so excited I can hardly wait! Invitation replies are pouring in thick and fast, and so far everyone has accepted, except for the Stubbs who left for New Zealand today! My dress is a *DREAM*!! Really a dream! I went along yesterday for the first fitting and let me assure you it is perfectly lovely – very simple and very young-looking. I hopped around to see if the top would slip down, but it seems firm enough so we're not bothering with bones. It is not at all *low* – and so there isn't that rather ugly expanse of neck, shoulders and chest that one often sees'...

One of the nicest things about Ralph is that *everyone* has a good word for him. Isabel has often told me instances of people who have come up to her and said, 'What a *terribly* nice man Ralph Watts is' – and 'Who is that terribly good-looking man who is so good at tennis' etc. etc. etc. Isn't it nice to hear things like that about one's friends? I really think I am the luckiest person alive at the moment to be having such a wonderful time! Just think – nearly 21 – gorgeous parents – heaps of friends – gay time in Baghdad and going home soon – tennis improving – new clothes – and Ralph. Who could want any more? I must stop romanticising – but it is such a heavenly evening and the light reminds me of evenings in Greece. How lucky I was to see that *lovely* country. Must stop now'.

Baghdad   *27 October 1951*

'...Ralph played his mixed doubles with Miss Stevens that afternoon and they won! They all had tea, and then the Jacquiers left them, and then they got up and went too. But Ralph came back (while she was changing or something) onto the lawn and came up to me and asked me about our match etc. and said, 'see you tomorrow'. I thought it was such a nice thing to do – as of course everyone had rather noticed him with Monica (that's her name!!). So I really don't think I need feel jealous – do you?!!

★   ★   ★

CHAPTER 9

Baghdad
06.11.51 - 27.12.51

Baghdad   *6 November 1951*

'Not long now – it is the eve of the great day!! I got your 157th letter at the Club yesterday, and thank you both very, very, much for all your good wishes etc. etc. and timely warnings about the 'affluence of incohol'. Daddy – thank you again and again for the cheque – it is a much better idea than sending something out, as I keep thinking of more and more things I'm going to want when I get home! At this rate I shall be a blooming millionaire – and be sending you and Mummy to Monte Carlo for the season!!! Anyway, thank you both again and again for *everything* – especially for being such wonderful parents, producing me, educating me, and above all letting me go about and see the world. You can't *think* how much I've learnt out here about people – and things. Above all I've quite decided now the *sort* of person I like and admire and wish to be like and vice-versa. Before, I was all in a muddle and wanted to do and be everything that anyone else was! I think you are quite the best, kindest, most generous, amusing and happy parents anyone ever had. Aren't I *lucky*!?!!

I must tell you of my cards, presents etc. so far. It's so exciting!!…*Such* a nice letter from Philip Mallet in England!! He had remembered and wished me a happy birthday etc. and said he hoped I'd have a 'thousand sons'!! I can't quite agree with him'!!!…

Baghdad   *8 November 1951*

'…The party last night was a most perfect climax to a very exciting day…I have never, never enjoyed myself so much or been so excited in my life…I have had simply millions of presents of every description…I just couldn't get over people's generosity, and George Newlands, who I was dancing with at the time said, 'Ah, we all love you, Mary'. *Nobody* could have had a better party – or a happier 21st…Now I must tell you all about it from start to finish…

Ralph arrived rather late – but wonderful to really have him *there*!!! I had a dance with him a bit later and he said he had a present in the car – but couldn't bring it in as it was a bit untidy! He wouldn't tell me what it was, but kept saying it was rather dull really and unoriginal. I couldn't think what it could be and then decided it might be nylons. Eventually I said could I go out and see it, and so we dashed out and there was this enormous box on the seat. I started to undo it – lots of paper and stuffing etc. – and it certainly wasn't nylons. There was a strong sort of rubbery smell – and you'll never guess what it was, I couldn't believe my eyes. A *WIRELESS*!!!! I just didn't know what to say or do – so didn't. It is a simply sweet little one – electric and very simple looking. Apparently you just plug it in, but Ralph is going to come along and fix it up for me. He says it will get a little out here – but in England it will be wonderful and I shall get *every* sort of programme I want from Europe etc. etc. I just can't believe that I've got a gorgeous little new wireless all of my own!! How *will* I get it home safely?!! Isn't it kind of him – I am just flabbergasted by it all. We went back and danced again and I could do nothing but *squeak*!

We had a most delicious buffet supper at about 10.30 or so and then danced and danced. At midnight Philip [Ray] lit the candles on the cake and they put out the lights and I had to blow them all out. Of course I didn't manage it all in one – but it was so exciting and everyone sang 'Happy Birthday' – and then to my horror yelled 'Speech'. I just said thank you to everyone and especially the Rays – and attacked the cake with great vigour to hide my confusion!! It was a delicious cake – all oozing fruit and lovely icing etc. and the decorations were *lovely*. Thank you very, very, much, Mummy. We danced on and on – and I thought my feet would fall off – but they didn't. Actually we all had left by 1.00 o'clock or soon after – so it wasn't really late – but *very* nice in fact. I think people were thinking of the Poppy Ball tonight – but I was rather glad as the Rays must have been exhausted. I went home with Ralph, clutching a zip bag with all my presents. He said I'd deserved it all – but I don't think I have!! Anyway it was a gorgeous evening and perfect ending'.

Baghdad   *13 November 1951*

'…My dear – believe it or not – I am in the FINALS of the Ladies Singles! I played Mrs Reed on Saturday afternoon and we were both at scratch which made it quite simple, but I didn't think I had a hope as she really is awfully steady. Anyway we played on the next-door court to Ralph, and the sight of him spurred me on. I won the first set 6-3, and then the second 6-2. I am still certain she had an off day or something! Anyway now I sit back until the finals are played'…

…Yesterday afternoon I played tennis with Mokhtar against the Peets (he is the Dutch Minister in Baghdad) and we had a good game. Mokhtar gave me some instruction in volleying from the net, which was useful. Ralph had asked me to play, but I couldn't and Monica Stevens was playing with him against Dennis and another man. We both ended our games at the same time, and Ralph asked me to come and swim – but I declined (bitterly cold!). However Monica swam I noticed –

and I hope she enjoyed it!! I had a simply gorgeous evening with Ralph and it has quite cheered me up now as I was just a teeny bit jealous of Monica (as she is stunningly pretty!), but actually I don't think I need worry now'!!…

Baghdad   *16 November 1951*

'…(Elizabeth and Robin have jut driven me from the sitting room and I'm now precariously perched on my bed!!). What an incredibly silly pair – they hummed and hawed for ages outside the front door, an then eventually came in and settled themselves down – so being a kind and tactful girl, I slipped discreetly (?!) away, falling over a stool and walking into a door that I thought was open and wasn't! Dignified exit! I intend going down for my supper soon anyway as I'm jolly hungry. Thank God Ralph isn't a fool'…

Did I tell you I've lost about three kilos and am now approx. 9 stone 8lbs!!? Isn't that grand!…

A pity Ralph had to go as I was hoping to see him – not having done so since Monday but I might ring him up a bit later and tell him the [tennis] results. I *suppose* it's alright, but somehow when I don't see him etc. everything gets depressing and I begin to worry and think he doesn't care. Do you think it's alright and are men like this?! He's simply gorgeous whenever I *do* see him, but it seems such a long wait between whiles. Still – I couldn't *bear* to be like Elizabeth and Robin who go out together every afternoon and evening!!…

I have just had my first French lesson – most encouraging'!!!…

Baghdad   *21 November 1951*

'…On Sunday I decided I would go to Matins for variety, and so I bussed and walked over – a lovely morning and really rather hot. It was a nice service, and we all had tea in the Padre's garden after. I then did some shopping and bought your things at Kashi's (a Persian dealer). I went home to lunch – and then flung off all my stockings etc. and wearing skirt, blouse and sandals, I set off for a mile-long walk. It was a perfect afternoon, and I took the ferry over the river and walked right down the far bank of the Tigris. It was quite lovely and I met a sweet old Arab who I talked to in Arabic – and he offered me a cucumber he'd grown. So I sat down and ate that, and then I was just starting back when I met Nigel Power – also out for a walk! He was awfully nice and asked me in to tea, but I wanted to get over to the Club, so I went into his house for a squash, and washed etc. (He lives in a lovely old Turkish house right on the river!). Then he despatched his boy to find a bellum [i.e. rowing-boat] that would take me over to the Club. One arrived, with a dear old 'Bellumchi' in it, who was stone deaf! So off we set – and I was quite sure we'd get stuck on the mud bank in the middle, but all was well, and he rowed me right over to the Club, which was grand. I arrived for tea, and luckily found Ralph who had finished his tennis etc. and took me home. He came in and we both had an enormous tea – toast and biscuits etc – which was rather fun. Then I had another early night, and felt much better on Monday'…

Baghdad   *29 November 1951*

'…I had my second driving lesson on Saturday afternoon – and practised stopping at 'crossroads' – the first time I slithered straight into the middle, but improved later! Then on Sunday morning I drove in 'traffic' for the first time'…

…I went to the Scottish dancing practice on Tuesday night – it was really great fun…Hugh turned up too and was *so* nice to me – I knew he must have had a certain amount to drink (Have learnt from bitter experience that people only pay me extravagant compliments in those circumstances!!). Anyway it was terrific fun an we danced and danced – and then Hugh took me home. He is awfully nice – but R.C. and a very touchy one! He is awfully clever though and interesting…

…Now I want your advice and *please* give it me quickly as I just don't know what to do, and of course have no-one to ask. I hate to keep on to Isabel and Elizabeth about it – and you should by rights be out here helping me!! I need you at this moment more than ever – but perhaps it's awfully good for me to have to solve all these problems myself! Anyway, just supposing Ralph is getting fond of Monica – what should I do? Of course I am *exactly* like Isabel over these matters and have a completely defeatist attitude. I would rather leave the scene of action *now* – before I get hurt too much – and then just try to get over it! I can't bear people to think that I am clinging onto him – and won't let go etc. etc. I would much sooner just give up – and let that be an end. Isabel agrees, but says that is why she thinks she hasn't got any further – because she always just gave up – and she thinks perhaps it's wrong after all. And yet, I can't agree with Elizabeth who is *so* different – madly attractive and has millions of affairs and yet has gone no *further* than Isabel!!! She, Elizabeth, would of course tackle Ralph quite openly and have a scene – quarrel or what you will. I *couldn't* do that as it seems rather fishwify, and perhaps (in my case!) a stupid fuss about nothing!! Now is the happy medium right? Shall I as I *feel* I ought to, just go on as though *nothing* has happened, be just the same, cheerful etc. etc. and not even hint to Ralph that I am jealous or that there is anything wrong? Then of course I sometimes feel that I don't give him any encouragement at all – he hasn't been to dinner since I got back from Greece – I went off on Sunday night to Hugh's – and of course I 'always' to him seem to be doing something I suppose. I daren't let him see that I care about him in case that should frighten him off – but perhaps I have been too careful to always do the right thing – and not to appear to chase him etc. *Perhaps* she thinks that I don't really care and have millions of boyfriends anyway – and at least Monica is fond of him etc. etc. It is a problem – but perhaps I have been wrong – as I notice Monica is much braver! Yesterday for example she was going back to the Railway Club to do old-fashioned dancing and Dennis asked Ralph if he was going too. Ralph said no, and Monica *immediately* said, 'Oh yes he will'!! And I expect he did as he hadn't been into the Mess when I rang up later!! Do write at once and console me and above all give me lots of sound common sense and advice on how to act. Oh! I wish you were *nearer*!! But until you do I am going to try to be very natural and cheerful and gay (jolly hard!!). Oh! dear – it's so easy to say but so hard to put into practice. The point is that I wouldn't mind who he took around in his car, played tennis with etc., if only I *knew* that he really cares about me. But I don't – how can I find that out? He might just be being 'very kind' to me, because I know how kind he can be but I wish he wouldn't to me. On the other hand it mightn't even have entered his head that I could think anything about Monica – but HOW CAN I KNOW?!! *That's* what's so awful – this not knowing – as he's never, never uttered a word about the future, seeing me in England or anything like that! And yet there's the wireless (my straw I clutch to!!) and the fact that he *has* taken me out all this time etc. and definitely no-one could possibly say I chased him to start with. Anyway lets hope tonight will be a big success – and I will write and tell you about it tomorrow! Please, please write soon and tell me what I should do? I hope this hasn't bored you stiff, but who else could I pour it out to?! I am sure it sounds quite hysterical and stupid, but it all seems madly important to me!! I suppose in 20 years when I am comfortably married to some fat old farmer or something, I shall look back and laugh!!...

P.S. You asked 'how far' Ralph has gone – not far enough is my answer'!!

Baghdad   *30 November 1951*

'Just to let you know that ALL IS WELL, in case you were depressed on reading my 157th yesterday!! However I still need your guidance and advice for future occasions!! I spent hours changing last night, and made a specially big effort – new brown dress etc. etc. etc., best new bracelet and all my 'glad rags'. Ralph arrived *long* before I was ready, so I was able to sweep into the sitting-room exuding Chanel No.5! Magnificent entrance!! Isabel was entertaining him, so that was alright. We finally went to the Club and had a drink in the bar first. Rather fun, as Peter Hawley is here for a day or two before going up to relieve Peter Jordan in the Ottoman Bank, Mosul. The latter has been transferred to the Sudan!! Anyway Ralph knew Peter Hawley slightly as he used to be here – so we had a long talk. Then Ralph and I had an excellent dinner – and saw the film which was quite amusing and then home – once more to the dying embers of a fire!! Anyway I have *no* fears now (at the moment) that he is even thinking of young Monica!! (touch wood and whistle!!). He was so nice to me – kissed me a *terrific* lot – etc. etc. etc. etc. And really I don't think I need fear anything now. He even commented that Dennis had fixed up this game again!! And we are going out to Baquba on Sunday as arranged – and also we are going to the British Club Dance on December 22nd together. What a relief it all is – and I feel years younger today. I could hardly sleep last night as I was so excited. Aren't I *lucky*?!! Anyway must stop now – it is the big Caledonian dinner and dance tonight – rather fun!

P.S. AIN'T LOVE FUN'?!!

Baghdad   *3 December 1951*

…'Now I must tell you all about my magnificent 'picnic' lunch yesterday! I had originally offered to produce the food part of it, but Ralph scorned my offer and insisted on doing it all himself. (I think he really wanted to show me how efficient he could be!). It was quite one of the most delicious lunches I have ever had – let alone just picnic lunches. Anyway, he collected me about 10.30 and we set off for Baquba – which is about 35 miles from Baghdad in the direction of Persia. It wasn't a very nice day and they tell me it rained quite a lot – but I didn't really notice! We had only got a little way when one of the sparking plugs gave out and so that had to be changed. All went well after that and we drove along quite happily through two little Arab villages to Baquba. It was a pleasant run – though the scenery is fairly uninteresting as it is very flat and bleak. However, the light was rather nice – the clouds were very dark and menacing but the sun came out now and again and made the ground very light and golden compared to the sky. (Ralph said that was the sort of light that Leonardo da Vinci used to like to paint in). We eventually reached the bridge over the Diyala (river – tributary of Tigris) and there had to go through the Police check. Ralph of course still hasn't got any number plates on his car, but instead had brought some cigarettes. However all was well and he told them that the car had been in Customs etc., and then gave his name etc. and also that his Mudir (Director) was Ibn Nuri Said (the son of Nuri – who is Col. Sabah, head of Iraqi Airways) – all this went down very well and then they looked in the car (at me) and said, 'Zawagatek' – which I knew very well meant 'Your wife?' Ralph said, 'Ee' (yes) and I giggled to myself because he didn't know I understood – and anyway it was the easiest way of explaining me!! We then had to give them our fathers' names which is the latest way of checking up if we are Jews or not! We parted with the Police on the very best of terms – many Salaams and cigarette smokings etc. etc. (How marvellous it is to be with someone who really can speak and understand the language and doesn't just bawl and yell and get angry in English).

We then got into the village of Baquba – which is most attractive, being typically Arab, but with a little stream running down beside the street. There were several ducks on it, and the odd woman washing her clothes at the bottom of the steps. We twisted and turned through the village until even Ralph had quite lost his sense of direction, not to mention me who hadn't even got a clue to start with! Our ultimate intention was to lunch on the banks of the Diyala, but we soon found ourselves on the road to Khanaqin – so had to turn back. We got back to where we first entered the town, and then, believe it or not, it was *me* who eventually found the ideal spot!! I knew exactly where the Diyala should be and so when I saw a little lane going left through the palms and orange groves etc., I suggested we should take it as I thought the river was at the bottom! Ralph said that the river was straight ahead and certainly not on our left, but anyway we could try!! So down we went and after about ¹/₂ a mile there was the Diyala straight ahead!! I *was* pleased with myself and Ralph was most surprised – navigation and all that!! It couldn't have been a better spot for a picnic as we were well away from the village and had no trouble with people coming along to have a look. (I think I must have inherited your instinct, Mama, for good picnic spots!). As it was raining slightly we stopped the car on the bank, and had lunch sort of semi in the car, overlooking the river – perfect!!

Ralph had been assuring me that he had remembered everything including the tin-opener – which he felt was terrific!! Anyway believe it or not the tin-opener turned out, after all that, to be a bottle-opener only!! How I laughed!! However, he managed to open all the tins most successfully with the plug spanner. Well – our menu – to start with there was half a cold chicken each – and quite deliciously tender. Usually the chickens out here are pretty stringy, but this one was quite delicious. There was a sort of tinned Russian salad to go with it, sandwiches and even a tin of sardines which we didn't even touch. Then for sweet two little tins of fruit salad and a tin of Danish cream!! Most exciting of all was when Ralph said quite calmly would I like red or white wine! I said white, thinking that he was joking!! Blow me, if he didn't produce a little bottle of Graves and one of Chianti!! Here we had another setback as the bottle opener – at least the corkscrew part of it – refused to open and the corkscrew unwound itself in the Graves cork!! So we gave that up and had the Chianti in teacups instead as that was a pull-out sort of cork!! It was a *gorgeous* lunch, and then we ended up with my coffee and biscuits and chocolate! This had all taken a long time, and unfortunately Ralph had to get back for tennis at 3.30. Of course he had been rung up on Saturday night (as a reminder only!) and had to say yes as he'd quite forgotten he was meant to be playing!! Anyway we went for a walk along by the river as we didn't have to leave until about 2.30 p.m. or so. I saw a simply *lovely* kingfisher – it had a black and white front and wings, with a magnificent bright blue-green back and we got really very close to it. There were lots of birds there, and I wish we could have gone on for a longer walk, but anyway there was the car. Ralph suggested that another time we will go out there immediately after lunch, and find someone to look after the car, and go for a proper long walk and take our tea instead. We took some photos, but I don't suppose they will come out very well as there was no sun. I took one of the river, and one of Ralph beside the car, and he took two or three of me – one with me beside the car. It *was* such fun. We had to drive back terribly quickly and of course even then Ralph was frightfully late for his tennis! He dropped me off and came back for tea after tennis which was nice'…

Baghdad   *7 December 1951*

'I am so fed up – there I was *terribly* cheerful for a whole week until yesterday afternoon – and now I'm back where I was with all the old doubts and worries!…

I had to play tennis with Bill Startup and the Moffatts yesterday – and it was pretty deadly anyway. But in addition, Ralph was playing with Monica…

The other *maddening* thing that has happened is that I've been asked to the Casuals' Ball by some *dreadful* young man from the Eastern Bank! I am absolutely furious. I was in the bank the other morning and Mr White, who is the Accountant, asked if I was going to the Casuals' Ball. It isn't until December 15th anyway – and I hadn't been asked yet, quite naturally, by anyone! Blow me if he doesn't go on about how 'slow' the young men are etc. etc. and how *dreadful* that I shouldn't have been asked. (He, incidentally, is selling tickets!). He then went on about how he'd asked 'the young lads in the bank' if they were going and they'd said no, because they hadn't anyone to take!!!…Agony and misery, however, in about two hours the phone rang and it was a 'Stewart Somers from the Eastern Bank' asking if I'd go to the dance. I hardly know him, and it was only by a process of elimination that I realised who he was by the name!! Of course I was absolutely caught and there was nothing for it but to say, 'yes'. Gosh! I could slay Duggy White. What makes me so mad is that he thinks it is *dreadful* if I'm not at a dance – …They just don't seem to realise that I'd a *thousand* times rather sit at home and get on with my book than go to these dances with ghastly boring people…Why should it always be me they pick upon? Then there's Bill Startup – 60 if he's a day – I am sick to death of it. Gosh! I am fed up. It's the old story – only senile old men, young boys and Iraqis (the latest addition!) seem to care about me…Ralph seems to have a once-fortnightly rule as far as I can see – and then all the rest of the time I am left to the tender mercies of these loathsome people...Probably the sooner I get home the better – or at this rate I shall be seriously considering becoming a nun to escape from it all'!...

Baghdad   *11 December 1951*

'...In the afternoon I walked for three solid hours all along the bank of the river on our side! It was simply lovely and a beautiful day. I saw two men ploughing by hand; one walked along digging with a long spade, attached to which was a rope; the other man walked down opposite to him and when one dug the other pulled with the rope – and they were in fact actually ploughing! I talked to lots and lots of Arab children etc. and took photos – and it was very pleasant'...

Baghdad   *14 December 1951*

'...My Christmas festivities to date are as follows. We stop work at lunchtime on Saturday December 22nd, and then don't work again until Thursday 27th! On the 22nd I go to the British Club Dance with Ralph in the evening, which will be terrific fun! Then on Sunday we have the carol service at 6.30 p.m. On Christmas Eve I had an invitation to a terrifying-sounding party at the Rendalls' – calling itself a Jamboree, and everyone is meant to prepare a song, skit or story or something to recite. Sounded too terrifying and ghastly for words, and so I delayed replying for a time. I found that Philip Mallet has also been invited and was slightly apprehensive, so he has asked me instead to go to the Christmas Eve Candlelight Dinner Dance at the Club, which sounds terrific fun. Anyway we are going to the Rendalls for a drink first, and then on to the Club. This was all fixed up after our tennis on Wednesday, and Adrian asked Isabel and so we will be a nice four. I am very pleased.

Then Christmas Day – so far we have Christmas lunch with Derek – and I expect that will mean the rest of the day. So that's alright! Then the next thing is the Embassy Ball on the 28th, which will be quite amusing, and then on New Year's Eve, Isabel and I are having a dinner party for all those non-fancy dressers! To date we have Margaret Oliver, our two selves, Ralph (very gratefully!) and Philip Mallet. We hope to have Hugh and possibly Nigel Power, and anyone else we find at a loose end'…

BAROMETER: V. HIGH
Baghdad   *18 December 1951*

'…The Casual's Ball wasn't too bad really! I spent most of the afternoon sleeping in preparation, and then I joined Isabel and Derek and Jimmy McKean for an early dinner at Hugh's house. That was very nice as Stewart Somers wasn't collecting me until 9.30 or so, which would have meant my having a cold and lonely dinner! We had some lovely red wine at Hugh's too, so when they deposited me back at the house I was feeling nice and warm and glowing! Stewart arrived and we went off to the Club, but as the dance didn't start till 10.00 we had a drink or two in the bar first. Then we joined the rest of the party which was composed as follows: a Mr and Mrs Watson – he is an adding-up machine engineer; and an Iraqi with a Scots wife; another half-Iraqi half-Scots who never opened his mouth; a young chap called Michael Wath (who is known as 'Flash Gordon') and he had a marked partiality for South American dancing – i.e. leaving one stranded in the middle of the floor for hours while he executed some type of native bonga bonga etc!; then there was Stewart and Stan Pele from Birmingham!! Anyway I was quite determined that at least I really would *look* as though I was having a whale of a time – and I certainly succeeded! Elizabeth said she really did think I was enjoying

myself, and Roger said yesterday that, I always look so full of
life it made him feel old!...

...I had dinner with Ralph again last night and we went to
the Railway Cinema. At last something constructive about his
future! He suddenly said he was definitely leaving Iraqi
Airways in June! You know his contract was officially up in
December? Anyway, he went to Tom Walters about it and both
agreed he couldn't leave now because Iraqi Airways would be
in rather a spot – and so Ralph said, 'could he stay on until
April?' However Tom said he must sign on for six months –
and so June it is. But he said he'd absolutely refused to stay on
for another year!!! So that is really rather satisfactory don't you
think? He gets three months leave when he gets home'...

Baghdad   *Christmas Eve 1.00 p.m.!! [1951]*

'...I had rather a shock over Philip Mallet the other night.
He was taking me home after we'd been to dinner at Arnold
Crowe's, and suddenly said he felt he owed me an apology
because he'd never said or done anything more after having
kissed me that time. I was rather taken by surprise – and before
I could collect myself he was talking away about how he didn't
know yet, and we ought to get to know one another better etc.
etc. etc. All very surprising as I didn't know he cared as much
as that!! Anyway, he must have started the 'getting to know me
better' part of it, as he rang up yesterday and asked if I'd like to
go out for a drive. So he came along after lunch and we had a
delightful afternoon. First we went out to see the Old Gate,
that is all that remains of the old Wall of Baghdad. It was blown
up by the Turks around 1917 – and now it has been turned into
a little armaments' museum, and we saw some old cannons etc.
I had been out there ages ago with Bill [Startup] when I first
came, but it is interesting to go back again. Then we visited a
very old building which was the old Customs House – by the

river. It is apparently the only remaining building of Haroun al Rashid's time – about 1500 or so I *think*. Anyway, it was great fun as we pottered through the suq – and then I asked Philip back to tea with Isabel and me'…

The British Club dance with Ralph was a roaring success…I asked him if he'd *really* enjoyed it – and he said he really had and that anyway he 'liked being with me – whatever the dance was like!!' Isn't that nice?!! Because that's how I always feel – couldn't care less about the dance if only Ralph is there. So it is all very nice and most successful!…I am very happy about it all now and only feel rather sorry for Philip who I must be *very* nice to'…

Baghdad   *27 December [1951]*

'…The Candlelight Dinner and Dance was very good in parts – like the curate's egg! The bad parts were when Ralph was dancing with Monica – who is a young flirt if you ask me!!! Also, Philip was rather a trial – as he would keep looking at me – and trying to dance close (Ralph said yesterday, 'Was he drunk?')…

After church we went along to see poor Nigel who was still in bed with jaundice! And then Isabel and I went on to drinks at the British Club…I then started talking to Mrs Brown (nice friend of Auntie's in Railways). She said she'd sat next to my 'boyfriend' last night (at the dance!) and that I must 'look out for that young monkey – Monica – and had I seen her snuggling up to Ralph?' (Had I not!!). Anyway, we chatted away about this – and eventually I said rather forlornly that I thought it was 'alright' really. She immediately said, 'Oh! yes – of course it is – in fact Ralph said so last night'. So I shrieked, 'How, when, why etc.' and apparently Mrs Brown had said something to Ralph about him picking the young and pretty ones etc.! And she said that he wasn't to forget 'the other one'.

And apparently Ralph said, 'Ah! Mary...' with great emphasis etc. etc. and Mrs Brown seemed to think it *was* alright – so I was greatly cheered up – had two sherries and a mince pie and felt fine for the rest of the day!!...

Hugh and I went out for a walk after lunch to get some fresh air – and it was very nice. We both agreed it was horrid not being at home for Christmas – anyway he asked me to go and see a film with him on Saturday night – which would be nice...He seems out of his element in the Rafidain Oil Company somehow and can't seem to settle on what he really wants to do'...

★   ★   ★

CHAPTER 10

Baghdad
02.01.52 - 15.03.52

Baghdad   *2 January 1952*

'…I am *terribly* sorry that Hugh is going on Saturday and I shall miss him in an odd sort of way. It was simply *freezing* in the cinema – although I had my thick coat on – and suddenly Hugh removed his raincoat and put it round my knees!'…

I have suddenly (within the last week!) begun to wonder if I'm still as serious as ever about Ralph. Perhaps it's a good thing if I'm not, because I promise you a few weeks ago I was quite certain that there weren't any more fish in the sea. I have been thinking about it a *lot* lately, and can't help thinking he's *too* perfect and self-sufficient to really want a wife. I feel he is the sort of man who wants to get married, have children, etc., sometime – and would like naturally enough a reasonable looking sort of wife. But I always have the feeling that he wouldn't really *need* one. I feel if I married him (and I'm sure he has no intention of asking me!) I wouldn't ever be any real use or assistance to him (except for children etc.) – and that he could get along equally well with anyone else. I would rather marry a man with a few faults who really desperately needed me – and who would perhaps be helped on his life by a decent sort of wife etc. etc. Oh! dear!! Can you get what I'm driving at?!

This isn't an outburst of jealousy or bitterness etc. that I felt a few weeks ago at all – in fact I feel particularly cheerful about the whole thing! But he *is* selfish in an odd sort of way, and I think perhaps it is because he has always got what he wanted

173

with little difficulty – and he is also very conceited. I can see now why Johnny (one of the most generous people in the world!) said he was selfish. He is rather aloof and taken up with all his interests, and unless one could and would be permitted to share those, I think life would be pretty bleak. Also I have noticed it over tennis – as he let it slip out one day that he thought Mokhtar was a fool always playing with his wife (who is only a beginner!) as it is making him much, much weaker etc. at tennis. Well – I think that's going a bit far if you don't want to play tennis with your wife in case you become less good! (Obviously one wouldn't want to play *every* day anyway). Perhaps someone nice and gentle and ordinary like John Clapp (just an *example*!) is better for a husband. Anyway I feel much, much better about it now that I have an open mind and I am not going to hurry – because I *am* only 21 and there are lots of fish in the sea…

P.S. But I do still like Ralph best!'

Baghdad   *7 January 1952*

'Today – as last – I actually play Mrs Boyce in the Finals. After all that she couldn't play on Saturday afternoon! Anyway yesterday if you please John Longrigg and I won the Embassy Tennis Tournament!!! It was a most amusing day. We started at 11.00 a.m. and had to play nine games against each other couple in the section. There were two sections each with five couples, which meant that we played a total of 45 games altogether. We played two of our matches in the morning, winning one and losing the other, but after lunch we won the last three and beat Mrs Boyce and a Mr Onslow 8-1 in our final match!!! (I hope it has shaken her morale for today). Anyway, our total games added up to 29 and that was the highest score in either section! However they had already prepared sealed handicaps, but we were lucky and were plus three, which brought us up to 32 and so tied with Philip Mallet and Biddy who had a plus eight handicap!!! So really we won the whole thing, before and after handicap. Anyway Biddy and I got brass elephant bells and the men brass ashtrays presented by Lady Troutbeck who came along with H.E. after lunch!! It was all highly entertaining and rather like a glorified Sunday School outing! We had lunch at 1.00 p.m. in the sun-lounge and of course ate an enormous amount! I declined curry and had stacks of cold meat and salad etc. instead, but I couldn't refuse the Christmas pudding! Then we had tea again when it was all over – and really we seemed to eat all day – the standard of tennis being quite appalling!!…

Ain't life fun?!! I feel *much* better now that I'm not *desperate* over Ralph! Quite carefree, gay and naughty in fact! However, don't despair because Ralph is still by far the best. (However, Isabel seems to be working up on the theme of Philip and I, as she says he is the nicest boy in Baghdad without exception!).

Baghdad   *10 January 1952*

'…Wasn't it dreadful losing my tennis against Mrs Boyce?! And of course it was just *pure* nerves. In the first set I couldn't hit a thing and there was a dull thud every time the ball hit my racket – and in the next I began to recover but too late! Still – it was all over in such a short time, and what does it matter anyway. I then watched Ralph and Monica covering themselves with glory beating the Mokhtars 6-0, 8-6! The entire Stevens family were watching, and I found myself next to Mama Stevens, who has an appalling cough, and would talk and cough into my left ear, telling me all about how Monica had never played in a tournament before although she had played for her school! I didn't tell her that I had never even played in any form of match until I came here! Then she suddenly said, 'Whoa! Mary'. So I suppose she has 'heard tell' of me!! When they finished playing, Ralph asked me to stay to tea but I was going to the Boyces' and couldn't…

I was going out to dinner at Philip Mallet's and he collected me…In fact it was a very pleasant evening and Philip brought me home about 12.30! Suddenly he said, as we were driving along, that I mustn't decide anything until I went back to England. He says I ought to go back to England and enjoy myself for about another two years before I make up my mind! I think he must have been thinking about Ralph as he said that he 'wasn't jealous' or anything, but that I just mustn't *do anything* before I go home! He says he wants to know me better before he makes up his own mind! (Oh! dear – what an awful muddle I'm in)…

…In the evening we went to the Gillibrands' Suki Yaki supper…And eventually we danced…I was quite glad when we left. I felt awfully depressed and dull and poured out my woes to Ralph, who was simply *sweet*. He said of *course* I wasn't dull, and said 'exactly the right things' and was sweet etc. etc. So I began to feel *much* better!! I said I thought it was time I went home to England and he said that I would leave 'a deep depression behind!' So I think it's alright, and I can't help liking him best. Oh! dear, isn't love *awfully* difficult?!! Anyway I shall take yours (and Philip's) advice and not 'do' anything in a hurry…

Baghdad   *25 January 1952*

'…I have got the most enormous stye on my eye I have ever seen – isn't it ghastly – and tonight is Burns Night! I refuse to go to the dance without an eyeshade…

…Tom Walters has been going on to [Ralph] about staying on – and I think he has pretty well got to now at least until *October* (misery!). They want to keep Ralph and not Treble (as he is more expensive, having marriage allowances etc. etc.) and also the Iraqis worship Ralph and everything. He still says he doesn't want to stay, but I think he will. Anyway if he does have to stay he says he will be home for a month's leave in May anyway…

…Isabel has now heard pretty definitely that she sails on the Baharistan on February 4th which means leaving Baghdad on the 3rd…

Baghdad   *29 January 1952*

'…The Burns Night was simply *terrific* fun – and in spite of my stye (I wore dark glasses in the end – Derek's bright idea!), it was quite one of the most enjoyable dances I've been to at the Club – for *ages* anyway!!…the speeches put everyone in a terrific humour as they were very good…I danced every *single* dance all evening. They were practically all Scottish dances… we got home about 3.00. But *everyone* enjoyed it and it was so spontaneous and nice…

I went for miles and miles along the river in 'Devonshire' on Saturday afternoon and had great fun talking to an Arab woman and watching her make khubz (bread). They just mix a sort of dough and then pat it out into large round flat cakes and plaster them inside round the walls of their mud-baked ovens. We chattered away – me in my two words of Arabic – and she offered me some 'Hashish'! I was rather shattered, but duly ate some – a sort of spinach – to discover afterwards that Hashish is the Arabic word for a sort of grass or vegetable – just as well! I also watched some men fishing – they go out in their boat and drag a net in a semi-circle to the shore – meanwhile a little boy bangs the water with a stick – and they then draw in the net and lo and behold there are about eight good-sized fish in 10-minutes – just too easy…

…Guess what I saw in the 'Tatler' of January 9th!! The marriage of Capt. John Michael de Burgh Ibbetson – 16th/5th

Lancers etc. etc. to a girl called Philippa Mary Heyland from Surrey. I saw his photo first – and giggled and giggled to myself. He was my big heart-throb – shipboard romance – etc. etc. on the *Empress of Australia*. Do you *remember*?!!... he was terribly fast, dashing, pleased with himself but *GORGEOUS*!!...

When I got back for lunch Philip Mallet had rung – and so I got on to him and he took me out duck shooting all afternoon – along the Baquba road. It really was terrific fun and we walked miles and miles over wet ground and Philip got a couple of teal and a gadwall (which is quite a large duck) – and we saw simply *masses* of duck. On the way home we saw (at least Philip saw!) some ruddy sheldrake and had a shot at them but missed. He wanted me to try to shoot some duck, but of course I always left it too late!!'...

Baghdad   *4 February 1952*

'Isabel left yesterday – and so Elizabeth and I are feeling rather lonely and depressed!...It was one of the worst days imaginable!! First high wind, and then of course dust, and eventually it turned into rain – mud rather – at about lunch time. *What* a day to depart on! Poor Isabel! Elizabeth and I gave a large lunch party at the Club for her – which was quite a good idea...We had an enormous curry lunch and then went back home to get Isabel off and packed up!! The last hour or so was pretty hectic as Pauline came in to 'help' – not a success – but we eventually got her down to the station and saw her off at 6.15 p.m. and what a crowd to see her off...

Hugh's coming back from Bahrain tomorrow. Isn't that *lovely*?!...

Baghdad   *7 February 1952*

'Isn't it *terrible* about the King? I didn't know anything about it, and when I went to the Club yesterday afternoon I asked why there was no film on Thursday and so found out. Poor Princess Elizabeth, and poor Australians being put off for the second time! But how nice that he just died in his sleep. We are working today as usual, although there was some confusion over it, and I gather we don't work on the day of the funeral. We had a choir practice last night, and apparently there is to be a huge service on the day of the funeral out here. Naturally everything is cancelled for a month, even the Padre's and Albu's concert on Friday…

The river is rising rapidly and I think we are in for floods like the first year I was here – but not quite as bad – people hope. Anyway it is meant to reach peak tomorrow night and Saturday, so watch the papers! Of course last year the river never rose at all. It is pouring down now from the north – bringing with it all sorts of flotsam and jetsam!'…

Baghdad   *9 February 1952*

'…We got the official Embassy staff circular yesterday morning and a nasty shock as all the ladies have to wear dark clothes until the funeral, and at the Memorial Service (Friday) we have to wear *black*. Of course, I haven't a thing except an evening bag, which Philip Ray suggested I should wear inverted on my head! But really I don't know what I am going to do – and I'm going to have a big try-on of Elizabeth's clothes this weekend. I don't want to have to buy anything out here though. Also we are not allowed to make *any* public appearance before the funeral – which naturally includes all parties etc., but also to my *fury* British Institute lectures, which I think is a bit much!! I got the first in on Thursday evening, but I was looking forward to next Tuesday's and Friday's when he [Robert Speaight] was going to read extracts from Eliot's plays and also Fry's and Shakespeare on Friday!…On Thursday it was a *most* interesting and comprehensive lecture on the revival of poetic drama in England – and the battle it is having. He told us a lot about T.S. Eliot's attempts – and his success with 'Murder in the Cathedral' and the others afterwards. Also, Christopher Fry – and drew our attention to the different methods and style of poetry. It really was terribly interesting, and of course he had it all at his fingertips – no notes – and knew just what he wanted to say…

…We had a good dinner and after motored up to Kadhimain and over the Bridge of Boats!! Rather exciting with the river so high, because now you have to go up onto the Bridge instead of *down*! And the water simply *tears* past the boats. The danger is lessening but I wonder whether this rain will increase it again – it has poured steadily since about 3.30 a.m. I believe!'…

Baghdad   *12 February 1952*

'…I had a lovely time on Saturday, in spite of it being a *vile* day! I went to lunch with Philip (and Robert McGregor) and it was very pleasant. On the way over Philip suddenly gave me a poem which he had written about me – or rather us!!!! I didn't know what to do about it – and I wish I was good at writing witty little verses in return. However I'm not, so I haven't made an attempt at a reply! We spent a very pleasant afternoon motoring around looking at the river etc. It was really *rough* on the Tigris and we watched a little boat absolutely rising and falling like the sea! We went through Kadhimain and over the Bridge of Boats again and then visited the Royal Mausoleum. I didn't think I'd be allowed in, but I covered my head with my mackintosh hood (like an Aba!) and they didn't mind at all. It is where all the members of the present Royal Family of Iraq are buried and was quite interesting. The main part is a large room – very high with a dome – and various alcoves off it all round where Kings Feisal and Ghazi, Queen Aliyah etc. etc. are all buried. Queen Aliyah's was lovely and a mass of fresh flowers (tulips, gladioli etc. sent daily by the Regent, but all the others were strewn about with the most *ghastly* dusty paper wreaths of artificial flowers! In one corner there were two mullahs chanting alternately from the Quran. I suppose they keep it up all the time…

…Anyway, Ralph was in the Club and we had tea and then off to Topas Khan to see the carpets. He is a sweet old man – Lebanese really – and he is trying hard to sell them before retiring to the Lebanon. It is rather sad really as he has collected carpets all his life, and the Iraq Government won't let him export them to the Lebanon. It was terribly interesting seeing them all, but needless to say I didn't buy any rugs! The only ones I really liked were some quite small Bokhara rugs (very good ones!) which I quite fell in love with. However, one was £70, and the other £63 – and both very small. However, they were beauties and it was fun just looking at them. I didn't like any of the cheaper rugs and so there was no point in getting one. However, it was fascinating and then he took Ralph and me into his study or sitting room, which was just one *mass* of carpets and rugs of all descriptions! Then there was a little alcove off it which he calls his 'Turkish room' – it was lovely – with old Turkish lamps and everything. He gave us some coffee and was awfully nice…

…I woke up on Sunday morning in *blazing* sun – and quite one of the most lovely days imaginable. (What to do?!!!). At first I decided to say I couldn't go with Philip, but soon changed my mind as it really was a perfect day for going out to Hindiya Barrage! So I rang up Ralph first – and before I'd begun even he said he knew just what I was going to say etc. etc.! So I thought this was rather odd, and of course he had to go to lunch with Donald Bennett to meet a BOAC official, had quite forgotten, and thought I'd remembered. So I giggled away to myself, but was *frightfully* honest and said that actually I'd rung up to say I couldn't come to lunch as I'd had the chance of going to Hindiya with Philip!! So all was well, and he said he'd been in fear and trepidation about ringing me. Anyway, he asked me to ring him back when I knew if I was going. So I then rang Philip and he said would I like to go and so that was all fixed up and he said he'd be round about 11.00 I then rang the Padre to give a message to Bill in church that I wouldn't be wanting my driving lesson, and finally rang Ralph again. He seemed very enthusiastic about it and said would I be going in the Humber?!! Of course he thought I'd meant Philip Ray and family – so I explained that it was Philip Mallet (meanwhile Elizabeth was in fits over the whole thing!!!). Anyway, Ralph said he wanted to hear *all* about it, 'every wheel turn' – so I am having dinner with him tonight! (Aren't I dreadful – is this playing 'fast and loose?!' Anyway, Elizabeth says competition is a good thing!!!).

We had a simply *lovely* day out at Hindiya and I felt so much better for it. I got some sandwiches, biscuits etc. and wore my oldest clothes – no stockings – and off we set. It takes about two hours to reach Hindiya, but is a very pleasant drive down the Hillah-Babylon road through Mahmudiya and Latifiya (where the Garbutts live) and then we turned right off the Hillah road through a village called Iskanderia (or Alexandria) and it is supposedly where Alexander died – as he died in or near Babylon! I saw two mongoose on the way, and lots of storks building their nests! We finally reached the Euphrates at a village called Musaiyeb and then straight down the river until we reached Hindiya. The Barrage is simply magnificent and was completed in 1914! It looked wonderful with the river so high and most of the gates were open and water just bursting out – masses of spray etc. I took lots of photos and hope they come out. We watched lots of boats going through the lock gates too – I have never seen it before and couldn't understand how it worked! Funny old-fashioned boats with high bows taking stones (for road-making) to Hillah and Kufa etc. They had their mud ovens built on the deck and were cooking their khubz in these when we were watching! For our lunch we crossed over the Euphrates and went upstream a bit. There were one or two gufas about (round coracles) and at least one of my ambitions was realised and we went in a gufa! You *must* remember to tell Mr Drury as it was he who told me all about gufas before I went out!! We just went downstream a little and then were hauled up again by a character on the bank. They are *very* buoyant as there was Philip, the fisherman, myself, Philip's gun and our lunch all in the gufa. They are rather giddy-making actually as you just spin round and round!! We had a lovely lunch – and it was gorgeously warm in the sun without being too hot. We didn't find any duck or geese for Philip to shoot, but stopped on the way back near Latifiya and shot partridges (only didn't get any!!). I took a photo of 'Philip-in-a-gufa' which I will send you as soon as I have finished the film'…

Baghdad   *17 February 1952*

'…Friday we dressed ourselves in our black (mine was most successful and lots of people said how nice I looked!!) and then off to the service. Of course I was shoved inside the church, being choir, but of course all the seats had been taken by then and I had an embarrassing few moments getting away from standing by the organ – where an 'usher' had parked me. After a long whispered argument with some man – I was persuaded to take his seat in the choir. Then I just sat watching everyone coming in. It was the most wonderful experience as there we were with every single foreign diplomat present – and every form of religion represented. We had lots of Moslems – and the head 'Naqib of Baghdad' – Moslem priest, Iraqi Cabinet Ministers and all the Diplomats, the Saudi Arabian Minister in all his robes and one in splendid sort of navy and gold uniform which I immediately took to be the Russian, but who turned out to be the French Minister! Then there were Armenian priests, Chaldean, Assyrian etc. It really was a most cosmopolitan congregation – and of course packed out and people standing. The service was relayed outside to about 300 more people – mostly Britishers. The service itself was excellent – very simple and impressive – two hymns and the 23rd Psalm – and an *excellent* address by the Padre. He was quite brilliant in what he said, or rather didn't say, when you consider *who* he was speaking to. Very tricky! Also, he spoke very slowly and evenly and it all came over the wireless beautifully although I didn't hear it recorded myself (it was on the European Service of the Baghdad Radio on Friday night)…

…Philip came round about 3.20 p.m. and we went off to Seleucia then. It was quite a long way and about opposite Ctesiphon! It was *terribly* dusty actually, and we arrived back about 7.15 p.m. just covered in dust from head to foot! My hair was all white literally and eyebrows etc. So it was just as well I hadn't been dashing out to dinner. We had a lovely afternoon though and saw all the mounds of Seleucia (nothing else remains) and bits of brick and pottery etc., but it must have been a large city as the area of mounds was very large. We walked down the river and talked and came back but it was mostly dark by the time we reached the main road again'…

Baghdad   *21 February 1952*

'…On March 1st our office is moving over to the Embassy, and thus the end of our independence! Nothing is changed really and our address etc. is all just the same, and it will be more convenient from the work and economy point of view, but *maddening* for us in that we have to do Embassy working hours, i.e. 8.30 a.m. – 1.00 p.m. and then *back* in the evening from 4.30 – 6.30 p.m. on Mondays, Tuesdays, Thursdays and Fridays! Not so good – but actually we can still play tennis in the afternoon – although it will have to be with a different set of people. Actually I suppose we shall get used to it, and anyway the others' summer hours start mid-April so it won't be too bad'…

Baghdad   *22 February 1952*

'…Yesterday was rather chaotic as I…still didn't know if Ralph was back or not. I rang the Mess once and must have got the cook who can hardly speak a word of English, because when I asked if Capt. Watts had been in to lunch – the reply was: 'cold steak and kidney pie'. Wasn't this *lovely*?!…

…Derek had rung in the morning to say that Hugh was back, but being *posted* to Kirkuk on Monday! *Very* sad, as I hoped he would be here now until I leave'…

Baghdad   *26 February 1952*

'So much has been happening in the last few days…What with Ralph, Philip, *and* Hugh!!

I will begin by telling you all about my 'lightning romance' with Hugh! I think I told you that when he arrived back from Amman on Thursday last he found he had been suddenly posted to Kirkuk for six months (as from last night!). Anyway, on Friday evening Elizabeth and I had round Derek, Jimmy and Hugh for drinks…Eventually they suggested we should all go to the Club for some food…and then finally we went off to Abdullah's about 11.30. It was great fun as I hadn't been there for *months* – and it was such fun with Hugh. He was terribly nice – and eventually I danced with him (not strictly allowed!), but we only had one although admittedly it continued for nearly an hour!…We all went home eventually – Hugh and I in the back of the taxi – Derek and Elizabeth in front – and poor Jimmy also in the back smoking a cigarette and looking out of the window!…I'd already decided to ask Hugh and Derek to dinner on Sunday night, as it was Hugh's last night…all went well – except that Abdullah Watchman never arrived to hand round veg. etc., so everything was even colder than usual!…We had a very nice dinner party and about 11 p.m. Tim Hillyard rang for a taxi and I wondered if they would all go. When it arrived Margaret and Derek both wanted to go home and so I thought that that was that, and they'd all go off and no more Hugh! However, to my surprise, he suddenly said, 'Do you mind if I stay and have another drink?' (Hoarse laugh from Derek – apologised for later!!) and so the others all left and Hugh asked if I minded. Of course I didn't, and he stayed until about 1.00 a.m.!! And I wasn't a bit tired, which was so strange. He said that he will take me to the Avon Valley Hunt Ball in two years' time *if* I'm not married (but he is quite sure I will be). Anyway he was awfully sweet, *terribly* nice and quite gorgeous, and asked me to have supper with him last night, before catching the train, but of course I couldn't as I was going to the music with Philip. Anyway he asked me to lunch, which was much nicer in a way as we were alone, and also it would have been terribly sad seeing him off, especially with everyone else there. He said he'd felt this coming for along time now, and I think I had too in a way! He seemed to know all about Ralph and just how things had been, as he said he'd noticed how miserable I looked on New Year's Eve, when Ralph had gone off dancing with Monica! I told him that I'd been pretty desperate about things then, but that I now felt much better and my heart restored to its proper place (or is it?!)…

I really think that this is the nearest I've been to really being 'in love' yet! Of course nothing will come of it now, as Hugh is in Kirkuk for six months (and can't get down again before I go) and then he still has another 18-months to do before coming home on leave. And he says I shall be married with two children by then – but he *has* said he will write, and I *hope* he will, but he is an awful correspondent and even Derek didn't have a word when he was in Bahrain. He said he loved me, and was 'fond of me' as well – and called me 'darling' and all sorts of things – but was *really* awfully nice and sweet, and shy, and not a bit fast type at all – please don't think that. He said he could never have kissed me on Friday night without having some drinks first, as he was much too shy, but he certainly managed it in cold blood after lunch yesterday!…

I had to postpone tennis with Ralph yesterday afternoon because of it all, and when I got in after shopping Ralph had rung me apparently and did so again at 7.00 just catching me before I went out. (He wanted to know 'what on earth I'd been doing with myself and why I'd dashed off to a lunch party', so I told him that I'd just had lunch with Hugh as he was going etc!). Anyway, he is night-stopping in Tehran tonight and said he'd bring back some caviar for dinner on Thursday when we are going to the Club cinema! Aren't I spoilt by my boyfriends?! We had a lovely afternoon on Sunday as he collected me about 4.00 p.m. and we motored out to the river Diyala on the way to Baquba and had a lovely picnic tea. We walked miles along the river and watched the sun set which was heavenly as it was a *perfect* evening. He rushed me back by 7.15 p.m. and I had a rush to be ready by 7.45 when Hugh arrived…

Before I go any further I must tell you what I haven't told to a *living soul* yet, and please for once, don't tell ANYONE about this, except Daddy, (because whatever happens I don't want to be one of those girls who dashes round saying she's had six proposals!). Anyway, the day we went to Seleucia – when we were sitting on the banks facing Ctesiphon (awfully romantic and historic) Philip suddenly said that he loved me, and that he *thought* he wanted to marry me (not for years anyway – so keep cool, calm and collected!!!). Anyway, I tried to tell him that at the moment I was very unsettled and that though at that precise moment I wasn't thinking of marrying anyone *else*, I didn't feel I was in love with him. (I tried to put it gently, but above all I feel I must be honest in these things). And so I think he realises now that I am not in love with him yet, but I know he hopes I will be. Oh! dear, I feel quite overwhelmed by it all at the moment, and even Ralph is being *far* more attentive. But in spite of all, I feel *so* much better in myself as at least I know that I am not in love with Ralph, or Philip (yet) and I don't think it's any good going on being in love with Hugh.

So I feel terrific – and in a way it's all rather amusing, except that I promise you I am taking it all seriously as I couldn't bear to hurt Philip especially. So I suppose in a way I've had my first proposal – not a bit as I expected and quite a shock!…

P.S. 12.30 a.m.!!!!…Derek informed me he is acting as 'agent'; he also says Hugh is the salt of the earth and would be difficult to beat anywhere even in U.K.!…Apparently he and Hugh had a very sombre little talk yesterday, and Hugh didn't want to go to Kirkuk now a bit and said, 'Why did it always have to happen like this?' He looked *miserable* at the station apparently and whispered into Derek's ear before he left, 'Give my love to you-know-who?' Derek is a *dear*…he is determined to fix up a trip north before I go and will give me a lift so I shall have to take a couple of days leave!!!'…

Baghdad   *29 February 1952*

'…Last night I had dinner with Ralph and then saw the Club cinema. It was fun and everything, but suddenly so *flat* after having been mad about him for nearly 16-months!! Isn't it funny how things work out, as I promise you if he had asked me to marry him up till two months ago, I would have said 'Yes' without any hesitation!! (I have come to the conclusion that he may be one of those odd men who feel they can't afford to marry, and that it will mean giving up so much!)…

P.S. Longing to hear your comments on Hugh! Daddy would like him very much indeed. He is tall – good-looking – brown hair – thinnish – *very* clever, went to Eton and Cambridge (or Oxford) and his father was something terrific! Our Ambassador in Tehran! (I do seem to go in for sons of Ambassadors don't I?!)'.

Baghdad   *6 March 1952*

'…I am taking two days leave…next Thursday and Friday and going up to Kirkuk by the night train on Wednesday and returning Friday night, to see Hugh…Derek has been *wonderful* and fixed up everything such as spending the night at the Railway Rest House etc. and all I have to do now is book the train…the Thursday and Friday is much better for Hugh as it is his weekend'.

Baghdad   *10 March 1952*

'Keep quite calm, but I leave Baghdad for good and all now on Sunday!! We are now due to sail from Basra on March 17th, so what about airing my bed?!…We should dock approx. 8th April…Incidentally you can't write to me en-route as we only stop at Kuwait to bunker (!) and then at Muscat, and *straight* home from there without any more ports of call…

Ralph is putting himself at my disposal on Sunday (the day we go!) and will rush me to banks etc. or anywhere I want to go, and if everything is calm and in order we are going for a quiet drive and picnic lunch. No final curry lunch for me – thank goodness! We leave on the train for Basra at 6.15 p.m.

It is all unbearably sad but luckily all so rushed that I haven't time to feel really miserable and anyway it is so madly exciting coming home! I get *so* excited when I think about it! Wow! Eeeee!'...

On the train to Kirkuk   *12 March 1952*

'...and I had a very nice dinner with Ralph. He really has been awfully sweet and nice lately and given up lots of his time to take me down shopping and going to odd places. We had an excellent dinner at the Zia Hotel, and the famous barman 'Jesus' was a great character. Ralph says he will be home for a month sometime in May, and asked if I could spare a few days to go and stay with them. It *would* be nice, wouldn't it, and he talked about hiring a car and taking me out in London and all sorts of *thrilling* things!! Anyway, I think it would be a good thing to go and meet 'Mum' and the family – don't you?'...

Baghdad   *15 March 1952*

'...I had a simply wonderful time in Kirkuk and the whole visit was a tremendous success from every angle. Hugh said that if I hadn't been going away for two years he would have asked me to marry him, but in the circumstances he didn't feel it was fair for either of us to get tied up so quickly and then have such a long separation. He asked me how I felt about it, and I was very relieved and said that I couldn't come to any satisfactory answer anyway at such a time – being all excited etc. over going home and everything. So our arrangement is very practicable. He wants me to go home and really enjoy myself and have 'lots of affairs' as he calls them, so that I can see if it really is Hugh or not. We are going to write to each other, and tell each other at once when we fall for someone else, and if, when he comes back, I am not married or anything, then we will meet again and see how we get on then! Anyway I can tell you *all* about it when I see you.

He was there to meet the train at 7.00 a.m. and we went straight to the Rest House and had an enormous breakfast and talked for ages. I had quite a nice room and it was all very nice and comfortable. Hugh had to work from about 9.00 – 11.00 a.m. so I sat by the fire and read my book – lovely, after all the rushing of the last few days. Also, it was bitterly cold up there and very wet and damp on Thursday. We walked into the town of Kirkuk on Thursday afternoon and up into the old part on the hill. We went into the Chaldean Cathedral, which was rather interesting. The Archbishop's house was just opposite. It seemed so funny to suddenly come upon this really quite large Christian church up there. In the evening we saw a film in Kirkuk, and then back.

Hugh came over to breakfast at the Rest House yesterday morning, and it was a lovely sunny day – the first for ages. So we set off with picnic lunch soon after nine in the office truck and went to Salahuddin! It was a simply lovely drive – miles and miles – through Altun Kupri and Erbil (at both places we stopped and drank 'chai' at the Rafidain Oil Co. filling stations while Hugh did a spot of 'work') and then up to Salahuddin. I went straight to the Evans' bungalow and found Margaret in feeding the baby…We eventually arrived back about six, and had dinner etc., and the train left (or was meant to!) at 9.00, but of course didn't leave till 9.40!!…

Well – now I'm all set for lunch with Philip Mallet, tea and photo with Ralph, and party tonight and off tomorrow!!'…

★   ★   ★

CHAPTER 11

The Journey Home – SS Nigaristan
18.03.52 - 18.04.52

S.S. Nigaristan – Just off Abadan   *18 March 1952*

'Well, here we are, anchored for two days in the river loading barley and dates as hard as we can go!…We sailed at noon yesterday and set off down from Basra with great gusto, and by this morning I thought we should have been far beyond Kuwait. However, about 4.30 we suddenly anchored to find that they hadn't been able to finish loading up at Basra because the water was too low, and so of course we have been stuck here since 4.00 p.m. yesterday, but sail at 6.00 a.m. tomorrow morning, with luck!! You can't think how fascinating cargo boats are – loading has been going on day and night, derricks and winches going non-stop – fierce looking coolies charging round. They slew a sheep on board yesterday afternoon and we watched them (just after our lunch!) skin it, remove *all* intestines etc. The 'scuppers' really *did* 'run with blood'. I can't decide whether I'm dreaming all this, whether we are back in the 18th Century, or whether this is 'Treasure Island' or what!!

We are called at 7.00 a.m. with tea and hot buttered toast (!), breakfast 8.30 a.m., consisting of cereal, fish and/or eggs and bacon, toast, tea or coffee. Coffee at 11.00 a.m., an enormous 3-course lunch at 12.30 p.m., tea and toast at 3.30 p.m., with a 4-course dinner at 6.00 p.m. That's not all – sandwiches and tea at 8.30 p.m., and after that we are allowed to relax our bloated and distended stomachs in slumber! Just expect a barrel to roll off the ship, and that will be me!…

Now to tell you about the events of the weekend. I had a

very nice lunch at Philip Mallet's on Saturday, and said my goodbyes to all the office people etc. and Lady Troutbeck in the morning. Ralph came dashing round about 5.00 and we tore down to town and had my photo taken. I wish I was there to see how they turn out, but he promises to send one for me to see! I tore back and went to see the de Courcys and then changed and put things ready for my party. Everybody turned up except Jim Woods, and it was a great success. We all drank quite a lot, but I left behind one bottle and a half of whisky and three full gins! *What* a waste! However, I bequeathed a bottle of gin to each of the Staff Houses, and the whisky to Mary and Elizabeth. We all of us went on to the Club for bar suppers – and *mercifully* no-one felt like going on to Abdullah's, least of all me. So really it was a *very* pleasant last evening and I was in bed by 12.00!! Poor Philip Mallet – Ralph rather took possession of me and took me home and everything, but I couldn't do anything about it anyway even if I'd wanted to! Ralph is much less worrying and troublesome than Philip. The next day when I came in at lunchtime I found Philip had called and left a lovely little Amara silver powder compact! Wasn't it *sweet* of him?! Oh! dear! I do feel sorry about him, and I *will* write and everything and try to explain everything…

…I have *never* seen such a crowd at the station in my life…The train drew out very, very, slowly and I couldn't believe I was leaving *all* those *gorgeous* people behind. Ralph and Philip seemed to be visible the longest!! However, I wasn't a bit sad or depressed (much sadder at saying goodbye to Hugh in Kirkuk!!)…Arrived at Basra, we just got into a speedboat and whizzed out into the middle of the river (Shatt al Arab) where the Nigaristan was anchored and there we were!!…It is all terrific fun, and I think I've got impetigo on my chin!!'

S.S. Nigaristan   *25 March 1952*

'...Now for the ship news! I am thoroughly enjoying the voyage and don't think I shall get too bored by England! We finally sailed again on the Wednesday morning after breakfast, and it was most interesting as we passed very close to Abadan and could see everything. My goodness – what utter fools the Persians are – there are all the buildings and installations quite idle now except for one chimney or so. It really was most depressing – not a tanker in sight – and the only sign of activity was Persians shooting round in the company cars. I took several photos and if they come out should be most interesting – in fact one might even make a bit of money by selling them to the 'Salisbury and Winchester Journal' at vast profit! You never know, they might be interested! The houses and gardens at Abadan looked delightful and certainly it was much pleasanter than I'd ever expected. We then passed Fao which is the big coming oil port for the Basra Petroleum Company, and will grow a lot I expect. Then we crossed over the Bar and into open sea – and down the Persian Gulf reaching Mena al Ahmedi that night at about 9.45 p.m. Mena is the oil port for Kuwait oil town (about 25-miles from Kuwait town) and we went right in there to get fuel. It was rather fun as we were towed in by a couple of tugs with much noise, poops and whistles!...We left Mena at about 4.00 a.m. and then set off down the Gulf until we reached Muscat on Saturday afternoon at about 3.00 p.m. We anchored in the bay and the other passengers and luggage and more dates etc. were all brought out by launch and boats. It is a most picturesque-looking place from the sea – high cliffs of dark rock surrounding the town, and a couple of forts built up the cliff by the Portuguese traders in 1585 and 1589 or so! It really did look lovely, but the 2/Officer told me that it is the hottest port in the world! It really is appalling in the summer as those cliffs just hold the heat and radiate it down. The temperature rises to about 103, and the humidity 98!! Ghastly! We collected four new passengers there…Our ship was surrounded by all the little boats – filled with faithful servants etc. bringing luggage, and also by one or two tiny canoes selling shells and funny little seed pearls etc. It was all most exciting and colourful – many of them being negro with fuzzy black hair – the influence from Zanzibar and Africa etc. This is a Sultanate – with a Sultan and all most feudal! It really is a most interesting place – and has quite a history, what with pirates and white slave trade etc! I spent most of the time we were stationary fishing from the bows of the ship! It was *so* exciting – the Captain produced a line (nylon) for me, a hook, and the ship's meat ration – and there I was. Would you believe it – but I actually caught a fish!! I was *so* surprised – it was only very little, but still my first fish, and caught at Muscat too!!!! By suppertime I had got the line into an awful muddle, but the 5th Engineer seeing my plight came and helped me unravel it and so saved me from the Captain's wrath!!…

It is terrific fun, and I have been doing some typing for the Captain! We all demanded jobs, and Philip [Ray] and Victor have been painting and varnishing every available thing on the passenger deck! I typed out passenger lists and crew lists etc. I have learnt all the crew names etc. We have a Captain, Chief Officer, 2nd and 3rd Officers, and then chief Engineer and 2nd, 3rd, 4th and 5th (my friend!) Engineers on board plus two cadets and then the crew are all Indians and the stewards are all from Portuguese India. Rather interesting as they are all Catholics and have wonderful Spanish names like: Gonsalves, Barretto, Fernandes etc. etc. Then a Seacunny who is a quartermaster who steers – and they have Lascars, Serangs etc., all of which I know the meaning now! The Captain has taken me all over the bridge, into the Chart Room and shown me everything – the echometer, and radar working. The other night I was hauled out of bed (9.15 p.m.!) to watch the radar working – it really is a marvellous invention. I have seen all over the boat deck and everything, and looked down on the engine room. It is all most interesting. The British crew are all terribly nice and rather amusing – the 3/Officer has been nicknamed 'heart-throb' (by Bridget!) as he has the most amazing side whiskers and also tartan socks! They are all from Glasgow, Ireland or Newcastle and great fun. I get teased from morning till night by the Captain and Chief and we have a most hilarious time at meals! I now sit on the Captain's right – place of honour – as the Chief has gone over to the other table with the newcomers. Mrs Harman has been placed at the extreme end of the Captain's table – he is scared stiff of her!! We are all getting on very well and Victor is extremely pleasant and the Rays, he and I have great 4s at deck tennis. We have organised a draw for the Lincolnshire Handicap tomorrow, and I have been typing out the lists etc. At 1.45 p.m. I've got to take down the runners in shorthand – rather frightening!! Most of the time we just knit, read, or gossip. Do you remember my blue pullover? Well, I have finished the back and the front and have started the first sleeve now. Wonder if I will finish it this voyage?!! I have only read three books so far'…

S.S. Nigaristan   *31 March 1952*

'…On Wednesday Mrs Harman woke me at 5.45 a.m. (!) to watch coming in to Aden. So I staggered onto the deck in my dressing gown and through bleary eyes watched us rounding into the bay…We got ashore to Steamer Point by about 11.00 a.m. and as we were sailing at 3.00 p.m. most of us came back for lunch at 1.00 p.m. I posted my 11 letters (total cost 11/11d!!) and then walked up to the main street, looking, being tempted, and resisting! In fact I only bought a film, some boracic acid for eyes, and two very pretty little white blouses embroidered in coloured silk…Aden town itself is about six miles from Steamer Point, and as you can buy everything you want there it didn't seem much point in spending 15/- on a taxi just to look at Aden town. I thoroughly enjoyed being ashore as it made a change, but there is nothing very exciting to see…

…I had been longing to see the engines etc., so the 5/Engineer was detailed to take me on a tour, and so we went down after dinner on Wednesday night – after Aden! (My goodness – I certainly chose the hottest night of the voyage as it is *much* cooler now). It was quite terrifying (and you would have loathed it) as we had to climb down flimsy iron ladders right down to the bottom! I had rubber soles on and, of course, slipped all over the place as the floor and ladders etc. in the Engine Room are all well oiled. However, we reached the bottom safely and I saw it all – into the boiler room to see the fires and the enormous boilers – then the piston which drives the propeller. The dear old 2/Engineer (aged 64!) was on watch and he came along and gave me a lump of cotton waste saying that I wasn't a proper engineer until I held some!! We then walked right along the propeller shaft to the stern and back. My goodness, the temperature was only 110 degrees F, but I was completely dripping by the time we got out and must have lost pounds that night! I had to go and have a shower and change completely. Actually they have ventilators which they can stand under when not actually working on the machinery, but even so the 5th said that the temperature goes up to 130 degrees in the Red Sea and Gulf in the summer! It was all beautifully clean down there, and what a change oil is after having to stoke the coal – that really must have been grim!…

…The Captain lets me sit up on the boat deck in a deck chair and get brown – very privileged aren't I!? I have been reading lots and lots of books…The other night the Captain took me up on the bridge and let me take the wheel. My goodness – it is a terrifying business trying to keep on the course set. I seemed to be spinning the wheel round and was quite sure everyone would notice the zig-zag course – but they didn't.

Oh! dear. Mrs Harman is dreadful – and of course I did what I didn't mean to last night – I got involved in an argument about the lifeboat numbers!! She really got terribly angry – and I didn't realise or I should have left it. Anyway she is in a murderous mood this morning and it is no good me apologising as I was dead right (checked with Captain). Talking of murder, Agatha Christie who knows Victor Rich quite well in Baghdad, is meeting him in London in May to get background information for her next year's thriller. It is going to be a murder on a Strick ship – and based on this voyage – with all names changed, but apparently she has never yet had a murderer on a boat. Rather fun – and of course I must get it next year!'…

S.S. Nigaristan   *7 April 1952*

'…What did I tell you – we are pulling into Algiers tomorrow for repairs to the bed plate which is cracked. (It is what the engine rests on!). Anyway the great discovery was made on Saturday when we were already past Malta, and so they thought they could make Gibraltar. However we are only going at seven knots which would take ages, and so the Captain has now decided to stop at Algiers for it to be repaired. It shouldn't take more than two or three days to repair, but of course it will mean we won't arrive until about 18th or 20th April! It's awfully annoying in a way, but so much better than arriving over the Easter weekend as perhaps you really will be able to meet me now, and of course my leave doesn't start until I land!! *Wonderful!*…

…We went up the canal by day, which is much the nicest,

and the Captain let me stay right up on the monkey deck (above boat deck!) all day. It was terrific fun waving and shrieking at all the soldiers – who yelled out 'Take me home to Blighty' etc. etc. We anchored for about three hours in the Great Bitter Lake opposite Fayid, and I took great delight in thinking how loathsome I had found it two years ago!! We were 17th in the convoy and had a Russian ship just ahead! We passed through Ismailia and eventually arrived at Port Said about 11.00 p.m. I had already gone to bed and sleep, but woke up on arrival and we all had our passports stamped in case of going ashore. However, it was no good as they were maddeningly quick with oil, water, and unloading etc. and we sailed about 6.00 a.m. next morning'…

S.S. Nigaristan   *8 April 1952*

'Oh! heavens. We've now heard on arrival at Algiers that the repairs are going to take at *least a fortnight.* Isn't it ghastly?!! Anyway, the captain has cabled his London office for instructions and it is *just* conceivable that they may trans-ship us – or let us go to Marseilles or something. Anyway, Philip Ray is going to notify our head office when we've heard from Strick's, as we couldn't take alternative route without their consent. He is all for staying put with our luggage unless we are actually ordered to leave the ship. So I will do whatever he does. He says they still can't count our leave until we actually land, which is something. Still I am rather fed up and bored'…

S.S. Nigaristan – Algiers   *Wet Easter Monday! 14 April 1952*

'…Algiers really is a lovely town – completely French of course – but beautifully clean and orderly with lovely big buildings. Everyone speaks French, and of course the town is filled with French people. I have seen lots of Arab women

though, with white abas and yashmaks! After dinner the first
evening Victor and I went ashore and had a walk round and I
was overjoyed to see some French Foreign Legion soldiers –
Beau Geste and all that!! I had to be hurried on as one turned
around, and seeing me goggling mistook my interest!…

We arrived back on board to find the agent, a cheerful young
man (married to a French girl!) who persisted in saying,
'Whack Ho' at regular intervals. He was amusing and a good
type. After dinner he took the Captain, Miss Ripton, and I
ashore and all round the town in his car. It was terrific fun and
we went right up the hill and saw the town and all the lights
below, called in at the St George's Hotel for a drink – a
heavenly place where Eisenhower had his headquarters in the
war! The flowers in the garden were heavenly and lilies just
grow *wild*! We drove miles around and talked for ages on the
headland by a Cathedral called Notre Dame d'Afrique.
Eventually we ended up in a night club on the Boulevard for a
drink. There, standing at the bar, was none other than Karl
Wolstrom – from the American Information Service, Baghdad,
having only arrived two weeks before! Wasn't it a lovely
surprise! The next evening he collected us about 6.30 p.m. and
took us up to the villa he shares with Tony Trotter – an ex-
naval type and at present agent for Ferguson Tractors. The
party was great fun – mostly French there – so I got some
practice! Tony should be on the stage as he is brilliant at funny
stories, and he told two in French which I understood!

Victor Rich and Mrs Boulter departed on Saturday morning
for Marseille, and we had a wonderful time up on the Monkey
Island yelling through the loud hailer and blowing the hooter
etc. etc. Never have they had such a send off!! Imagine them
arriving at Victoria now – all in Easter Monday rush! I didn't go
ashore on Saturday but prepared myself for Easter – much hairwashing etc.

…Tony Trotter collected the Doctor and I and took us for

the most wonderful drive westward along the coast to see the 'Tomb of the Christian Girl', which is Roman, about 2000 years old and really rather interesting. We went right inside along pitch dark passages. We stopped at a café on the way back to collect buns and then called in on a Group Captain and Mrs Butts who had very kindly asked us in for drinks. We brought Tony back on board and had a most entertaining evening in the bar! He really is a character and has an inexhaustible fund of naval stories etc.

…I have just written to Ralph and Hugh as it's such a foul day'…

S.S. Nigaristan, Algiers   *18 April 1952*

'…You must think me perfectly awful, not accepting the alternative route, and for that reason I didn't even mention it in my letter as I didn't want you to get the wrong idea and think I didn't *want* to come home! However, since you've heard from Stricks – that is that!! I was going to tell you about it when I saw you, so that I could explain properly. Anyway that second afternoon, Victor and I arrived back on board to discover a 'council of war' in progress. Stricks has phoned from London to say that passengers could, if they wished, fly straight to London (Air France) the next day or as soon as passages could be got – or stay put and forever hold their peace! Anyway, I found Philip straight away and told him what the form was. He said at once, 'Stay put' – so there we are. I must say it would have been pretty ghastly packing up everything and leaving it all behind, and just arriving with a suitcase! Anyway, Bridget said that they wouldn't have let me fly off alone on Air France. Philip wrote to Head Office next morning informing them we had been delayed owing to engine trouble for two weeks – but not mentioning alternative route (so for heaven's sake don't breathe a word to anyone – you know how things get around!).

Anyway, Philip says he couldn't possibly have transported children and everything home by air – and anyway it is nothing to do with the Office as it is *Stricks* who offered alternative route, therefore it is nothing to do with the Office who already agreed to our sea-travel, taking luggage with us…

How simply *WONDERFUL* about Michael [Clapp] coming home. I thought he wouldn't be back until September. I am so looking forward to seeing him again – and how nice of him being at Greenwich next winter!!'…

Hugh wrote too on 27 March, and Philip on 30th – neither had had my letters! Lovely, as that means I ought to hear again soon. Gorgeous letter from Hugh – he is a dear. And also Philip who was sweet – and says he is 'behaving perfectly normally now that there is nothing he can do, and eating like a hog'. I am *so* glad – awful if he had pined away!!!!!

I had a simply lovely day yesterday (weather perfect) – leaving on a bus tour at 8 a.m. We went along the coast road to Tipasa and saw the Roman ruins – such a lovely situation, overlooking the sea and most interesting. A rather boring Frenchman who I was sitting next to in the bus insisted on giving me lunch at the café – I must say it was very nice as we had two hours to wait – vin rosé, soup, fish, meat, cheese and fruit!! After lunch we visited the Roman Tomb again, and then right across to the mountains and up a lovely gorge to the Ruisseau des Singes (Monkeys' Stream!). There, when the bus stopped, I saw to my surprise Hind, the agent!! He was a perfect beast and looked straight through me (on purpose!!), making me think I was seeing his double!! He had brought Pippy and the Captain all the way to meet me because he had your two letters for me!!! So your letters came 60 kilometres to be delivered!!! Wasn't it fun though, and was I glad to speak English again! Gosh it had been a strain. I left the tour, and we all came back together – such fun. They had only decided after lunch to come and 'rescue' me, and had a breakneck drive to the Gorge to get there in time!! We were far too late for 6.00 dinner, so we four had supper in the Captain's day cabin – great fun!…

Hoping to see you in about a week's time.

Fondest Love,

Mary'.

★   ★   ★

The Casuals Ball at the Alwiyah Club.

The Hindiya Barrage.

Ralph Watts and his MG at Baquba.

The Rev Granville Borlase (with Pekinese) and Ralph Watts.

'Devonshire' farms on outskirts of Baghdad.

Philip in a qufa at Hindiya.

Suez Canal. Statue of de Lesseps, Port Said.

Endpiece

Philip Mallet finished his second tour of duty in Baghdad over a year later, and was posted home to the Foreign Office. He and Mary married on 28 November 1953. They have three sons, and (so far) eight grandchildren. Sometimes they quarrel loudly about loading the dishwasher.

Wedding picture.